HERMES BOOKS

John Herington, General Editor

Also available in this series:

Homer, by Paolo Vivante (1985)
Pindar, by D. S. Carne-Ross (1985)
Aeschylus, by John Herington (1986)
Hesiod, by Robert Lamberton (1988)
Ovid, by Sara Mack (1988)
Horace, by David Armstrong (1989)
Virgil, by David R. Slavitt (1992)

CATULLUS

CHARLES MARTIN

YALE UNIVERSITY PRESS
NEW HAVEN AND LONDON

874.1
C36zm

Set in Palatino Roman types by Brevis Press, Bethany, Connecticut. Printed
in the United States of America by Vail-Ballou Press, Binghamton, New York.

Library of Congress Cataloging-in-Publication Data

Martin, Charles, 1942–
    Catullus / Charles Martin.
    p.   cm. — (Hermes books)
    Includes bibliographical references and index.
    ISBN 0-300-05199-9 (cloth). — ISBN 0-300-05200-6 (pbk.)

    1. Catullus—Criticism and interpretation.   2. Verse satire,
    Latin—History and criticism.   3. Love poetry, Latin—History and
    criticism.   I. Title.
PA6276.M37   1992
874'.01—dc20   91–40354

The paper in this book meets the guidelines for permanence and durability
of the Committee on Production Guidelines for Book Longevity of the Council
on Library Resources.

10   9   8   7   6   5   4   3   2   1

to my mother
KATHLEEN

and to the memory of my father
CHARLES

*so that you shouldn't imagine your words had been scattered
to the aimless winds, put from my mind and forgotten*

CONTENTS

FOREWORD *by John Herington*   ix
PREFACE   xiii
ACKNOWLEDGMENTS   xv

Part I   *Buried Presents*

    I   "THE VERY WORST OF POETS"   3
   II   THE BOOK OF CATULLUS   26
  III   LIFE INTO ART   37

Part II   *Poetic License*

   IV   OF POETRY AND PLAYFULNESS   67
    V   INVITATIONS AND EXCORIATIONS   92
   VI   TRANSFORMATIONS OF THE GIFT   121

Part III *Vanishing Lines*

  VII   ON PASSIONATE VIRTUOSITY IN A POEM OF
        SOME LENGTH   151
 VIII   LIFTING THE POET'S FINGERPRINTS:
        A READING OF POEMS 61–68   172

        NOTES   187
        BIBLIOGRAPHY   191
        INDEX   193

FOREWORD

"IT WOULD BE A PITY," SAID NIETZSCHE, "IF THE CLASSICS should speak to us less clearly because a million words stood in the way." His forebodings seem now to have been realized. A glance at the increasing girth of successive volumes of the standard journal of classical bibliography, *L'Année Philologique*, since World War II is enough to demonstrate the proliferation of writing on the subject in our time. Unfortunately, the vast majority of the studies listed will prove on inspection to be largely concerned with points of detail and composed by and for academic specialists in the field. Few are addressed to the literate but nonspecialist adult or to that equally important person, the intelligent but uninstructed beginning student; and of those few, very few indeed are the work of scholars of the first rank, equipped for their task not merely with raw classical erudition but also with style, taste, and literary judgment.

It is a strange situation. On one side stand the classical masters of Greece and Rome, those models of concision, elegance, and understanding of the human condition, who composed least of all for narrow technologists, most of all for the Common Reader (and, indeed, the Common Hearer). On the other side stands a sort of industrial complex, processing those masters into an annually growing output of technical articles and monographs. What is lacking, it seems, in our society as well as in our scholarship, is the kind of book that was supplied for earlier generations by such men as Richard

Jebb and Gilbert Murray in the intervals of their more technical researches—the kind of book that directed the general reader not to the pyramid of secondary literature piled over the burial places of the classical writers but to the living faces of the writers themselves, as perceived by a scholar-humanist with a deep knowledge of, and love for, his subject. Not only for the sake of the potential student of classics, but also for the sake of humanities as a whole, within and outside academe, it seems that this gap in classical studies ought to be filled. The Hermes series is a modest attempt to fill it.

We have sought men and women possessed of a rather rare combination of qualities: a love for literature in other languages, extending into modern times; a vision that extends beyond academe to contemporary life itself; and above all an ability to express themselves in clear, lively, and graceful English, without polysyllabic language or parochial jargon. For the aim of the series requires that they should communicate to nonspecialist readers, authoritatively and vividly, their personal sense of why a given classical author's writings have excited people for centuries and why they can continue to do so. Some are classical scholars by profession, some are not; each has lived long with the classics, and especially with the author about whom he or she writes in this series.

The first, middle, and last goal of the Hermes series is to guide the general reader to a dialogue with the classical masters rather than to acquaint him or her with the present state of scholarly research. Thus our volumes contain few or no footnotes; even within the texts, references to secondary literature are kept to a minimum. At the end of each volume, however, is a short bibliography that includes recommended English translations, and selected literary criticism, as well as historical and (when appropriate) biographical studies.

Throughout, all quotations from the Greek or Latin texts are given in English translation.

In these ways we hope to let the classics speak again, with a minimum of modern verbiage (as Nietzsche wished), to the widest possible audience of interested people.

John Herington

PREFACE

THE PRESENCE IN THIS SERIES OF A BOOK ON CATULLUS MAY RE-
quire some justification: it was, after all, a classicist who noted
some years ago that "the common reader has been enjoying
Catullus behind the scholar's back."[1] Though his remark un-
intentionally brings to the mind's eye the image of a ménage
à trois that surely would have delighted the Latin poet, we
must restrict ourselves to dealing with that remark in the sense
in which it was no doubt intended: is Catullus already sufficiently familiar to—if not with—the common reader? Have we
here a poet who needs no introduction?

The answer, as so often with Catullus, is yes and no.

He is, to be sure, the most popular of Roman poets, widely
read both in his own language and in numerous translations,
almost proverbially accessible, appealing to us by virtue of his
passion, his wit, and the immediacy with which he delivers
both to us. I think that it is fair to say that *this* idea of Catullus
is the popular one. It is not wholly inaccurate, but it is far from
complete: there is another aspect of the poet's work, less accessible and more in need of an introduction.

Catullus is not just a poet of unimpeded spontaneity and
uninhibited self-expression: however minor many of his
poems may be, they exist in complex relations with one another, with their subjects, and in a dynamic tension between
their formal elements and their often informal utterances. Catullus is a masterful ironist practicing a highly sophisticated
art, and both in his minor pieces and in his major work—the
long poem at the center of his collection—the poet's intentions

and accomplishments have much in common with those of our modernist and late-modernist masters. To say that about him is not to dismiss Catullus the lyricist and satirist but rather to offer the common reader access to the art, the artifice, and the matchless intelligence behind the maker's impassioned intensities.

ACKNOWLEDGMENTS

THIS BOOK GREW AROUND A TALK GIVEN AT THE INVITATION OF McGill University's Classics Club in the winter of 1978. It contains a few pages from an essay of mine published in *Parnassus: Poetry in Review,* and a poem that first appeared in *Poetry: A Magazine of Verse* as "Lines Freely Taken from Callimachus."

The influence of Gregory Bateson's essay "A Theory of Play and Fantasy" is everywhere apparent in my chapter "Of Poetry and Playfulness." "Transformations of the Gift" owes much to a timely encounter with Mikhail Bakhtin's *Rabelais and His World.*

The Djerassi Foundation provided me with periods of residency, remembered with gratitude, during the writing of this book. I am also grateful to the PSC-CUNY Research Foundation for a Creative Incentive Award in 1986.

All of the translations of Catullus to be found herein are from my version of *The Poems of Catullus* (Johns Hopkins University Press, Baltimore, 1989); I would like to thank Eric Halpern, editor-in-chief, and the press for permission to reprint.

Finally, I wish to thank the general editor of this series, whose learning I have leaned upon and whose abiding concern for clarity of thought and accuracy of expression, percolating through draft after draft of this book, did much to make it better.

I BURIED PRESENTS

I "THE VERY WORST OF POETS"

Pessimus poeta let him remain. He can afford to be elbowed out of the hierarchy of Roman literature, for he scarcely belongs there.

—Eric Havelock

WHEN I BEGAN READING LATIN POETRY AS AN UNDERGRADUATE, it seemed to me that the classics could be represented as a series of uncompromisingly realistic ancestral busts, a succession of gradually diminishing likenesses worn ever smoother by the piety of generations, receding in an unbroken line that ended at some distant, featureless, almost unimaginable urstone. Like ancestors of the Roman kind, the classics made a daunting prologue to the present: secure in their own accomplishments, they were not at all shy about proclaiming them, not at all eager to make way. Here, for example, is Horace, firmly putting modesty aside as he heralds the accomplishment of his third book of Odes:

> I have completed a monument more lasting than bronze, loftier than the regal pyramids; devouring rains, the fierce north wind, the numberless years as they pass by one after another, even the very flight of time itself will be helpless against it.[1]

Reading Horace, I was an awed but skeptical provincial at the base of that monument, hesitantly deciphering its unfamiliar text. That voice could never be mine: its accents were the accents of revelation. Reading Catullus, however, was an altogether different experience, for what emerged from his text was the voice of a contemporary:

> Si qui forte mearum ineptiarum
> lectores eritis manusque vestras
> non horrebitis admovere nobis

3

If any of you happen to be future
readers of these trivial absurdities,
and find that you can touch us without bristling

[14b, 1–3]

Here diffident, but elsewhere brash, intrusive, unbuttoned: it
was impossible to think of Catullus as one of the classics. Poets
like Virgil and Horace, the real classics, fit in, but Catullus was
clearly something else. I wasn't quite sure what else, but it
seemed natural then to think of him as one of the moderns, if
only by analogy to such writers as William Carlos Williams,
Ezra Pound, and Henry Miller, whose work I was beginning
to dig into, and who likewise tended toward the brash, the
intrusive, the unbuttoned.

At any rate, I knew it would be pointless to look for Catullus anywhere along my imaginary row of sculpted faces: to
have located him accurately, I would have needed an altogether different model of history. Such a model was close at
hand, if I had only realized it. During the time that I was reading Catullus, I also read *The Gold of Troy,* Robert Payne's
popular biography of the German archaeologist Heinrich
Schliemann. When Schliemann dug into what turned out to
be the site of Troy, he found a jumble of golden masks and
broken crockery, abandoned gods and goods that spoke of the
irreparable shattering of quotidian certainties. Only a paradigm that arranged time vertically rather than horizontally
could have made sense of what he found there: the present lay
on the surface, and the past was literally underfoot; older was
deeper.

The model that Schliemann constructed from his labors
continues to inform us: it represents, in the words of Clifford
Geertz, "not history as a continuity, one thing growing out of
the past and into the present, like the chapters of a nineteenth-
century romance. It is a series of radical discontinuities, rup-
tures, breaks, each of which involves a wholly novel articulation of human observation, thought and action. . . . The past
is not prologue; like the discrete strata of Schliemann's sites,

it is a mere succession of buried presents."[2] That understanding of history is one which we recognize as distinctively modern—as modern as the thought of Charles Darwin, Sigmund
Freud, or Michel Foucault, the subject of Geertz's sentences.

It also offers us a model of time in which we can locate
Catullus, for, despite his modern habit of turning up in the
company of the classics, he and his generation represented just
such a radical break in the continuity of Latin poetry. Formally
innovative, intellectually and emotionally sophisticated, Catullus and his colleagues created a poetics of the subjective,
the ironic, the erotic. To their contemporaries, who referred to
them in Latin as "the new poets" (*poetae novi*) and in Greek
as "the modernists" (*hoi neoteroi*), it must have seemed as
though these writers, known today as the neoterics, had come
out of nowhere, for they were almost without precedent in Roman literature.

We can admit Catullus as a modern poet by allowing the
possibility of the inexplicable appearance of the unprece-
dented and the novel in any age, but is this too facile an analogy? Were Catullus and his neoteric associates modern in the
same way that our modern poets were? This is not an easy
question to answer for a number of reasons, not the least of
which is the assumption of unanimity of enterprise among the
great modernists of our recent past, an assumption that we
perhaps have an easier time making now in their absence than
we would have had when they were among us. Nevertheless,
there were similarities between these ancient modernists and
ours. It is perhaps best to begin with the most obvious of those
shared characteristics that they and we can recognize as modernism. What seems to me indispensable to the modernist experience, and an area shared by our modernists and by the
neoterics as well, is the idea of modernism as a radical change
in the nature of the relation between the intentions of the artist
and the expectations of the artist's audience.

Where poetry is a customary art, the poet will have an
audience, the audience will have its expectations, and few will

be seriously concerned with the question of what poetry is, for it will generally be assumed that it is that stuff which satisfies the expectations of the audience for poetry. It will be written from the poets' experiences and in language that can be described as "poetic"; and while there may be some disagreement as to the precise meaning of that term, few if any will doubt that some experiences are poetic and some are not, just as some kinds of diction are poetic and others are not. Poets will be free to alter their experiences to bring them into conformity with the received opinions of the day about what is acceptably poetic, and questions about their sincerity will not be raised. Certain metapoetic utterances will make no sense whatever, and will seem at best to be merely provocative. The concluding couplet of Archibald MacLeish's "Ars Poetica"

> A poem should not mean
> But be

is an example of the kind of aphorism which almost no one before the early twentieth century would have thought very useful, had anyone been able to understand it.[3]

In such a situation, the balance between the intentions of the artist and the expectations of the artist's audience is clearly weighted on the side of the audience. However, where poetry is not customary, or where the customary kind of poetry is being challenged or overthrown by another kind of poetry—that is, where the poets are in revolt against what they perceive as the strictures imposed by their audience—then the balance tilts in the other direction, and the intentions of the artist become paramount, while the expectations of the audience are neglected. This state of affairs, whether it occurs in the United States in the early part of the twentieth century or in Rome during the first century B.C., is necessary for, if not sufficient to, the development of something recognizable as modernism. Wallace Stevens annotates the abruptness of the revolution in his poem "Of Modern Poetry":

The poem of the mind in the act of finding
What will suffice. It has not always had
To find: the scene was set; it repeated what
Was in the script. Then the theatre was changed
To something else. Its past was a souvenir.[4]

And when the poet is no longer content to repeat what is in the script, there arises a problem of definition, for what, after all, is poetry? If the audience is sitting on its hands, not knowing what to expect, or if it is indignantly filing down the aisles and out of the theater, then the poets may feel even more free to substitute their own intentions for the no longer useful expectations of their audience. Poetry now becomes what the poet means it to be, a projection of individual intentions: the poem of the mind in the act of finding what will suffice.

Among what remains of the audience, there will be considerable confusion about what is and is not poetic, and even about whether it serves any purpose to attempt such a distinction. The question of the poet's sincerity will gain new currency, and in many cases sincerity will come to be equated with the obscurity of the poetry and the isolation of the poet. Certain metapoetic utterances, such as MacLeish's couplet, will quicken with new relevance. For it will be reasonably maintained that, if one cannot have both meaning and being at the same time, it is more urgent to have being than meaning even if, around the edges of that assertion, there hovers an anxious little question: Urgent for whom?

In a culture rich enough to support more than one kind of poetry, it is possible for poetry that satisfies the expectations of its audience to coexist with poetry that ignores those expectations. In our own time, for instance, a truly bewildering variety of poetries compete for the divided attentions of those readers few but fit. In 1912, however, poetry still had a large general audience, and its expectations were handsomely met when Edwin Marsh published the first of his annual anthologies of Georgian poetry. Two years later there appeared Ezra

Pound's rival anthology, *Des Imagistes,* a book that brought together a number of poets whose subsequent work and influence would radically alter a great many widely held notions of
what poetry was in our time. Nevertheless, Ezra Pound could
not have prevented that eminent Georgian, Walter de la Mare,
from offering his readership such diversions as he did in such
poems as "All That's Past:"

> Very old are the woods
>> And the buds that break
> Out of the brier's boughs
>> When March winds wake,
> So old with their beauty are—
>> Oh, no man knows
> Through what wild centuries
>> Roves back the rose.[5]

No one would ever doubt what is here expressed in lines to
which no one would ever object, though a poet on the modern
side like Pound would no doubt have found the alliteration
comical in its earnestness, the *oo*ing and *ow*ing rather mechan-
ical, the syntactical inversions stultifying, and the sentiment
insufferably banal. If we find ourselves in agreement with that
assessment, it is most likely because the intentions of Pound
and the other Imagists have become part of our own expectations for poetry. For many of De La Mare's numerous admirers, however, the work of Pound and company simply
could not have been considered poetry. Pound's "L'art, 1910,"
cited in its entirety, will give an idea of the gap between the
two camps:

> Green arsenic smeared upon an egg-white cloth,
> Crushed strawberries! Come, let us feast our eyes.[6]

Pound and the other modernists succeeded in driving
away much of the audience that existed for poetry when they
imposed their own bold intentions on the way of settled expectations. They knew perfectly well what they were doing,
and what the consequences of their actions would be: if one

grows up reading Longfellow, one grows up expecting few
aesthetic or moral surprises. If one reads William Carlos Williams, one finds, at first, little else. In 1920, Williams dished
out some real guff from an imaginary reader:

> I do not like your poems; you have no faith whatever. You
> seem neither to have suffered, nor, in fact to have felt any-
> thing very deeply. . . . There is nothing appealing in what
> you have to say but on the contrary the poems are posi-
> tively repellent. They are heartless, cruel, they make fun
> of humanity. What in God's name do you mean? Are you
> a pagan? Rhyme you may take away but rhythm! why
> there is none in your work whatever. Is this what you call
> poetry? It is the very antithesis of poetry. It is antipoetry.
> It is the annihilation of life on which you are bent. Poetry
> that used to go hand in hand with life, poetry that inter-
> preted our deepest promptings, poetry that inspired, that
> led us forward to new discoveries, new depths of toler-
> ance, new heights of exaltation. You moderns! It is the
> death of poetry that you are accomplishing.[7]

Ears grow walls when expectations are defied. Williams
clearly understood that the business of being modern involved
a paring away, a deliberate diminishment of the resources
available to poetry, resources he saw as no longer relevant to
the art; along with that diminishment went a dismissal of the
now irrelevant expectations of the audience. Furthermore,
Williams understood that his audience would perceive this
stripping away not simply as a necessary part of the process
of aesthetic renewal, but rather as a willful and inexplicable
rejection of shared moral values. The poetry which he was la-
boring in isolation to create would be perceived by the general
audience as a fundamentally immoral art.

Having almost no audience at all in 1920, Williams was
forced to invent one, an appropriately solitary soul who would
respond with outrage to his destructive accomplishment. Neither his situation nor his strategy was entirely without pre-

cedent. Circa 55 B.C., Gaius Valerius Catullus wrote the lines
I quoted earlier:

> If any of you happen to be future
> readers of these trivial absurdities
> and find that you can touch us without bristling
>   [14b, 1–3]

Williams conjures up an imaginary reader no longer able to
expect the kinds of moral and aesthetic nourishment that poetry once provided. For Catullus, the situation is apparently
even more desperate, and he seems unable to imagine an audience that will not be unrelentingly hostile, that will not bris-
tle like boars, shuddering at the very touch of his poems. This
is clearly a comic exaggeration, but with equal clarity, these
three lines make two straightforward assertions: there are at
present—his present, that is, not ours—virtually no readers,
and the possibility of there being any readers in the future
seems highly doubtful. The explanation for this unsatisfactory
situation perhaps appears in the word Catullus uses to describe his work, *ineptiarum*. The poems in question are absurdities, unsuitable for the serious readers of his day or ours. In
the poem that now appears as the first of the entire collection,
we find another version of the theme of neglect:

> To whom will I give this sophisticated
> new chapbook, just now smartened up with pumice?
> To you, Cornelius! You had the habit
> of making much of my poetic little   [1–4]

There is at least one reader, and no doubt there were others.
Here Catullus describes his poems as *nugae*, trifles, a self-
deprecating assessment quite in keeping with the attitudes of
Greek and Roman poets about this kind of poetry. Nevertheless, in this dedicatory poem and in the three-line fragment,
Catullus is clearly saying that his poetry did not enjoy popular
success. Whether he is describing the situation accurately is
another question; it is clear, however, that he wants us to be-

lieve this. And if it is true that there was little public acceptance of the kind of poetry that Catullus was writing, the most likely reason for this is that his intentions were opposed to the expectations of the audience of his age.

Although that audience and most of its literature have long since vanished, enough is known about them for us to be able to recreate, at least in general terms, the expectations prevailing in the time of Catullus among those for whom literature was important.

The earliest Roman poetry was not self-consciously literary at all: it seems to have consisted of such folk forms as hymns and ballads, as well as short dramatic pieces performed at religious festivals; in all likelihood, little if any of it was ever written down. The word customarily applied to it by literary historians is "rude." And rude it no doubt came to seem to the Romans themselves, for they knew that they were cultural parvenus living in the shadow of Greek achievement. Although the Romans might have looked down on the Greeks as deficient in manly vigor, they nevertheless looked up to them as superior in cultivation of the civilized and civilizing arts. By the middle of the second century B.C., the Romans had begun to import Greek culture in its most movable manifestations: works of art and those who created them. And if some Romans looked on that art as nothing more than a way of ornamenting their leisure, others turned to the task of creating and nurturing a national literature based on the most appropriate models they could find, exhibiting in this enterprise the same kind of dedication that they customarily displayed in public affairs.

What the Romans wanted were the classics in paraphrase, and so the models that they turned to first were the older Greek forms of epic and tragedy. A certain Livius Andronicus, active between 240 and 200 B.C., translated the *Odyssey* into Latin, using the traditional Latin meter, the Saturnian. Andronicus was a Greek prisoner of war, a slave who was serving as tutor to the children of a powerful Roman family, and his version of the *Odyssey*, retrospectively revered as the first step in the development of a national literature, was a text intended primarily for the education of Roman schoolboys.

The unelevated social position of the man considered the father of Roman literature was anything but anomalous in the Roman world. The nobility had better things to do with their time than scribble verses. They commissioned plays, but they most certainly did not write them: slaves could—and did—do that. Typically, whether slave or free, the poet was dependent upon a patron, usually a socially prominent member of a distinguished family, who supported the poet in exchange for translations of Greek plays that could be performed at religious festivals, or for poems celebrating the glorious deeds and illustrious career of one or another member of the family. Where these poets were not slaves, they seem to have occupied a social niche similar to that occupied by contract Hollywood screenwriters in the 1930s: slavery, in some instances, might have been preferable. In our post-Romantic culture, poets are reckoned to be independent, even of their patrons, should they enjoy the favors of such an anachronism. This kind of independence was unknown to a Roman poet, who would never have been so bold as to consider himself one of the unacknowledged legislators of the world; he knew only too well that he was the servant of the world's acknowledged legislators and that his task as a poet was to embody and promote their values in his verse.

By the time of Catullus, this situation had changed to the extent that the nobles had given themselves permission not only to attend the theater but to write for it. They might also attempt to dazzle the company at table with erotic or satiric epigrams. More important, however, those well-to-do young men who, like Catullus, were inclined to the study and practice of literature and had the wherewithal to pursue their inclinations now had the opportunity to devote themselves to their art in a serious way. Nevertheless, the patron-client model of literary production persisted. Although he was financially independent, Catullus was part of the circle surrounding Gaius Memmius, just as the financially dependent poet and polemicist Philodemus of Gadara was a member of the circle of L. Calpurnius Piso.

The archaic Roman poets who followed Andronicus imitated the Greeks in meter as well as in matter. They quickly abandoned the native Saturnian meter of early Roman poetry as too rustic to capture the sophisticated brilliance of the new Greek models. The subsequent metrical history of Latin verse can be seen as an attempt to adapt Greek quantitative measures (based on syllabic length, rather than on stress) to the Latin tongue.

With the exception of the comic poets Plautus and Terence, these earlier Roman poets are now no more than names attached to fragments, but by translating Greek tragedies and comedies into Latin and by composing dramas set in their own time and on their own soil, they advanced the project begun by Andronicus. The poet Naevius wrote the first epic on a Roman theme, the *Bellum Punicum,* which dealt with the protracted struggle between Rome and Carthage. The most influential of these early figures was Quintus Ennius, the first Roman man of letters: critic, translator, author of comic and tragic dramas, and—most important—author of a historical epic, the *Annales,* which traced, in myth and history, the development of Rome from the arrival of Aeneas in Italy to the events of the poet's own time. When Catullus began writing, an appreciation of Ennius was one of the hallmarks of conservative poetic taste.

From the moment it began to take itself seriously as literature, Latin poetry had been dependent on Greek models. That relation of dependence continued through the time of Catullus, when the Romans turned their attention from the older epic and dramatic forms of Athens to the new and more sophisticated models imported from Alexandria. Nevertheless, some of the Romans must have felt that they were adding to their sources something that was not present in the originals. Ezra Pound's view of the matter is worth noting: "We may suppose that the Romans added a certain sophistication; at any

rate, Catullus, Ovid, Propertius, all give us something we cannot find now in Greek authors. . . . Ovid indubitably invented
and added much that is not in Greek, and the Greeks might
be hard put to find a better poet among themselves than is
their disciple Catullus. Is not Sappho, in comparison, a little,
just a little, Swinburnian?"[8]

The poets of the formative age of Roman literature created
a body of work that married Greek forms and Roman vigor.
Their influence extended well into the time of Catullus, and
their work created its own expectations in the audience for
whom they wrote. Poetry, as they understood it, was very
much a public affair, both in its concerns and in its reception.
It took the form of epics or panegyric odes recited in public or
of dramas that were meant for public performance at religious
festivals, and even when comedic, poetry was a serious, high-
minded enterprise. The comedian Terence complains that the
Roman audience was not quite up to the sophistication of the
comedies that he wrote for them.

Fusing myth and history, this literature taught the offspring of Romulus and Remus the lessons of their past and
instructed them in how they were to live in the present, in full
consciousness of their noble destiny. And so, when Catullus
looks to the future hoping for the readers lacking at present,
readers who will not be scandalized when they pick up his
poems, it is most likely this larger audience that he has in
mind; raised on a literature of high purpose and serious nature, that audience would not, or could not, accept the kind of
poetry that he and his crowd were bringing into existence.

Rome was, after all, a cultural backwater, where the
weight of tradition was far heavier than we can easily compre-
hend. When Catullus began writing poetry the dominant
literary influences in Rome were the comic tradition, represented by Plautus and Terence, and the epic-tragic tradition,
represented by Ennius. Whether or not Catullus felt indebted
to them as precursors, they could not have provided him with
models for the kinds of poetry that he and the other neoterics
were interested in writing.

There had been at Rome an apparent precursor of the neoterics: the poet Laevius, who lived and wrote during the first quarter of the first century. Little more than a name today, Laevius survives only through the title attributed to his work and an assortment of metrical scraps (including one complete poem); that title, *erotopaegnia*, and the bits of his work that have survived, suggest that he was a direct forerunner of Catullus and the neoterics. As A. L. Wheeler wrote: "Laevius composed a series of poems in lyric meters which are called by Porphyrio 'lyrics' and are cited no less than eight times by Gellius and others as *erotopaegnia*, or 'erotic playthings.'"[9] The sensual light verse of Laevius heralds the Catullan model, as Wheeler states: "The rather numerous fragments prove that in many ways he was striving to work along the lines which Catullus and his contemporaries followed."[10] These short poems in lyric meters investigated erotic subjects and employed fantastic neologisms in a spirit of playfulness. Wheeler cites as an example of his word play *subductisupercilicarptores* and notes that "this sesquipedalian compound, 'naggers with lifted brows,' is at once a contemptuous reference to his critics and an exaggerated example of one of the points for which he was criticized. He stuck to his guns."[11] Catullus would most certainly have known his work, and if he had judged it, as modern critics do, to be polished verse but crude poetry, it could not but have made an impression on him.

But if Laevius had been radicalized, this was due to the influence of contemporary Greek poets, who, in Alexander's wake, were just as likely to come from an out-of-the-way place like Gadara as from Athens. Their poetry was influenced by that of the earlier Alexandrian poets, who had begun to flourish at about the time that Andronicus was translating the *Odyssey* for the edification of Roman schoolboys. The Alexandrian influence, however, does not seem to have been felt in Rome until the last years of the second century, in the generation that preceded Catullus.

In the work of the Alexandrians, and especially in that of the poet Callimachus, Catullus and his generation discovered much of interest. However curious some of its literary products

seem today, the neoterics must have found in the Alexandrian
sensibility almost the perfect antidote to the established Roman tradition. The most appealing characteristics of that sensibility seem almost to contradict one another: on the one
hand, a spirit of playfulness responsible for producing our first
"concrete" poems—verses that, when they were written
down, took the shape of an altar or the pipes of Pan; on the
other hand, an equally Alexandrian self-consciousness, a
sense of cultural belatedness: everything, as Callimachus complained, has already been done.

One could know this only if one already knew everything,
and the Alexandrians were not averse to giving the impression
that they did: what else can account for a monograph *On Words
Suspected of Not Being Used by the Early Writers*, or a catalog (in
120 volumes) of the *Tables of Persons Conspicuous in Every Branch
of Learning and a List of Their Compositions*? And in uneasy co-
existence with this impulse toward the encyclopedantic, there
could be found as well a counter-impulse to compress the
world into two or four lines of verse: epigrams as concise,
witty, and even raffish as their learned monographs were ex-
pansive, dry, and sober. Here is a somewhat free rendering of
a streetwise transcription of a brief colloquy between a co-
quette and her customer by the Syrian love poet Philodemus:

> He: Yo, Missy?
> She: Talking to me?
> He: If you're not busy . . .
> She: Why wouldn't I be?
>
> He: Dinner?
> She: Am I invited?
>   Dinner'd be nice.
> He: And after?
> She: Delighted!
> He: So'm I! Your price?
>
> She: Nothing up front,
>   I'll let you decide:

> Give what you want
> When you're satisfied.

He: Oh, you *are* clever—
　　But when? Noon? Nine?
She: Whenever. . .
He: Now?
She:　　　　Your place or mine?[12]

The Greek original consists of only three elegiac couplets in the course of which there are twenty alternations of voice.

　　The Alexandrian concept of the poet was one that the neoterics found congenial: the *poeta* was *doctus*, erudite in his knowledge of his tradition and sophisticated in his understanding of poetic technique. But it was the Alexandrian respect for technique and appreciation of concision which were their most important gifts to the neoterics. In the surviving preface to one of his lost works, the *Aetia*, Callimachus defends both virtues from poets and critics who prefer natural bombast to artful intelligence. The poem that follows is once again a translation as a Roman would have understood translation—freewheeling, but faithful to the spirit of its original.

> Some enemies of mine (and of the Muse)
> Recently having learned to tie their shoes
> And toddle upright, scarcely ever falling,
> Have now decided on a brand-new calling:
> They will be critics! And it's me they're after!
> "He's not a poet—just an arts-and-crafter:
> Two lines a week, tediously diminished,
> Until his tiny masterpiece is finished.
> He's the one who's finished: nothing left to say,
> No epic grandeur, no grant from the NEA."
> But I learned my art from divine Apollo:
> "Here are two rules that I would have you follow:
> When you are sacrificing, choose a beast
> Almost too fat to waddle to the priest,
> For fatty meat is always sweet and tender.
> But when you're singing, keep your muse slender,

Your lines melodic and your thought compressed:
Leave thundering to Zeus—he does it best."
I've done so all my life. And now today
When bombastic bards belligerently bray
For asses' ears in poems called profound
By those who only weigh them by the pound,
I think of the sacrifices that I've made,
All of the fat trimmed by Apollo's blade
And see no need to change: the god was right.
My lines stay green although my hair's turned white.[13]

Public taste may not have been as sharply divided between the old and the new as Catullus implies. Cicero, who championed the older literature, seems nevertheless to have had a keen interest in the new work and its practitioners, referring to the neoterics three times in those of his own writings that have come down to us. Two of his remarks deal with fine points of neoteric practice, indicating that whether or not he read the neoteric poets with approval, he certainly read them closely.

Cicero knew their work then, and knew at least some of them, including Catullus, and Catullus' friend Calvus, with whom he engaged in an extensive correspondence, two volumes of which were known in antiquity. A single letter from either of those lost volumes might tell us a great deal more about the ancient modernists than we now know. One of the things we might have learned is whether, when Cicero used such terms as *neoteroi* and *novi poetae*, he was referring to a specific and clearly defined group of poets, as we would be in referring to the Imagists or the Movement; or whether, in fact, he meant by those terms an entire literary generation, as we would be in referring to "the Beats," for example.

There is no way to say for certain that the neoterics constituted a school of poets as we would understand it, but certainly the evidence from Catullus' own poetry, in the form of polemic and apologia, suggests the existence of a tightly knit coterie. Its members included Licinius Calvus, equally distinguished as poet and orator, and Helvius Cinna, mistaken, after the death of Caesar, for the conspirator Cinna and torn by the mob for his bad verses, as Shakespeare has it. Their work exists only in fragments. Other poets mentioned by Catullus, and usually considered part of the group, are Valerius Cato, Cornificius, and Furius Bibaculus. More ghosts: Nothing at all has survived of Cato but his reputation for having been very influential as a poet and critic, while Cornificius is reduced to bits and tatters, and Furius Bibaculus has been spared total oblivion to the extent of two not very interesting poems. No doubt there were other poets associated with the group in one way or another. There is, for instance, the Caecilius who would have been absolutely unknown if his friend Catullus had not sent him poem 35:

> Go, poem, pay a call on Caecilius,
> my friend the master of erotic verses:
> tell him to leave his lakefront place at Comum
> & spend a little time here at Verona,
> for I have certain weighty cogitations
> to deliver—words from a friend of ours!
> —Wherefore, if he is wise, he'll eat the road up,
> although a thousand times his peerless lady
> should seize him, fling her arms about his neck, and
> beg him to linger in her soft embraces.
> That girl is crazy for him; if the story
> I've heard is true, she perishes of passion:
> for ever since she first read his unfinished
> poem, his epic Mistress of Dindymus,
> flames have been feeding on her deepest marrow.
> Lady more artful than the Sapphic Muse is,
> I feel for you! It really is exquisite,
> his almost finished poem on Cybele.   [1–18]

And there was also the poet and polemicist Philodemus of Gadara. It is not possible to prove that he was part of Catullus' crowd, but his literary concerns were similar to those of the neoterics.

But what were those concerns? We are accustomed to our modernists' having programs that they defend and promote in manifestoes; ours is an age in which the ideas that surround a work of art are often at least as interesting as the work itself. It may be that somewhere in the lost letters of Calvus to Cicero there existed the equivalent of a "neoteric manifesto." In the absence of any reliable document, however, I have been put to the trouble of forging one of my own, based on a similar document concocted by Ezra Pound and F. S. Flint at the instigation of Harriet Monroe, who wished, in 1913, to explain Imagism to the readers of her new magazine, *Poetry*:

The Neoterics

The neoterics denied that they were a revolutionary group; however, they readily admitted that they were a school, one in which poets might make themselves familiar with the best models of the past, among whom they include especially Callimachus and Sappho. They seemed to be absolutely intolerant of all poetry that was not written in such endeavor, ignorance of the best tradition forming no excuse. When asked if it were not true that they had in fact been influenced by Ennius and other Roman antecedents, they very quickly changed the subject. They had a few rules, drawn up for their own satisfaction only, and they had not published them. They were:

1. Whether lyric or epic, a poem should directly express the personality of the poet. Playfulness, sensuality, and erudition are characteristics as valuable in a poem as they are in a friend or lover.

2. There is no point in redoing what has already been well done. With specific reference to the possibilities of the EPIC, we do *not* need another Homer: what we *do* need are poets doing what Homer didn't get around to doing.

3. *"Mega biblion, mega kakon."* Poetic merit is most often found in inverse proportion to the expansiveness of the poem under consideration: briefly put, concision is a virtue. The national impulse to drop a monument at the sight of a laurel wreath has already been sufficiently well exercised by Ennius, Hortensius, Volusius, et cetera.

4. "Sheer plod makes plough down sillion shine": technique, i.e. a concern for it, for its own sake, is NOT to be despised. That much, if nothing else shd. be self-evident.[14]

Subjectivity, novelty, concision, and polish in verse: four aesthetic concerns that had not previously furrowed the Roman brow are now very important, at least to Catullus and his colleagues. The notion that a poem should be the expression of the personality of the poet is not to be found in traditional Roman poetry, in which the personality of the poet is subservient to the Greek text he is translating, or to the story he is telling, or to the *patronus* who is paying his way. This new notion gave poets the license to experiment with lyric forms, but it also allowed them to alter the traditional concept of the epic as well. The earliest Roman epic, the *Bellum Punicum*, had been an expression of the will of the Roman people, and exalting their national purpose in the saga of founding and nurturing the state had become the traditional theme of the epic. For Catullus and his circle, it was an exhausted notion. They conceived of an epic in which the audience's traditional expectation of grand scale, of heroic purpose and action are thwarted by the poet's insistence on diminution and intensity of expression, his interest in seeing the action from inside, as it were, exploring his own subjectivity as he explores the subjectivity of his characters. The revelations of this kind of epic are personal and erotic in nature. In poem 95, Catullus hails the arrival of just such an epic, written by his friend Cinna:

Nine years ago Cinna first began work on his epic,
    and nine years later—at last—the *Zmyrna* is ready!

Meanwhile Hortensius was churning out five hundred
  thousand
. . . .
The *Zmyrna* will be read on the banks of Cyprian
  Satrachus,
  the very ages will age, perusing the *Zmyrna*;
while the *Annals* Volusius wrote will die by *their* river,
  the Padua,
  a cheap and all too abundant wrapping for mackerel.
                                                    [1–8]

The prediction made by Catullus did not, alas, come true, for
only three lines of the *Zmyrna* survive. Its subject was suitably
erudite: the hapless passion of Zmyrna for her father, Cynyras.
After being metamorphosed into a tree, she gave birth, from
her trunk, to Adonis. In praising Cinna, Catullus takes a swipe
at Hortensius for his lack of concision and at Volusius, whose
title suggests that he was an imitator of Ennius, for his lack of
originality. (Catullus thrashes him in another poem for his lack
of craftsmanship.) The nine years of labor to which Catullus
refers are perhaps not an exaggeration: the neoteric insistence
on technique and concision must have made the longer forms
a time-intensive labor.

The emergence of such concerns among the neoterics is
no doubt a consequence of the group's participation in the critical dialogue about the nature of poetry which had gone on
from the time of Plato.

Plato's belief that poetry was both inaccurate as a representation of reality and so seductive to the emotions as to be
socially dangerous was answered by Aristotle's defense of poetry as an imitation of nature, an expression of the universal,
whose effects on the soul were both morally improving and
educative. Aristotle's argument was subsequently taken in two
directions: the Stoic philosophers looked on poetry as an agent
of moral education, while the Alexandrians saw it as an
instrument of pleasure. The Alexandrian poet and critic Era-

tosthenes said, "Every poet aims at charming, not instructing." Every poet—not just, as we might imagine, the lyric
poets. His polemical remark must be understood in the context
of a situation in which claims for a certain kind of poetry are
being advanced, no doubt against a competing kind. Nevertheless, in denying any educative purpose for poetry, the remark also removes it from the sphere of shared experiences
and values and makes it subjective, a purely personal concern.
We are educated into a body of common knowledge, but the
music which sends me into raptures may put you to sleep, or
drive you from the concert hall with your hands over your ears.

If poetry has educative value, then, a critic must take this
into account when judging it. The epic poet cannot be considered without reference to his ability to provide us with heroic
role models who show us how we should live our lives. Proof
of the didactic poet's greatness is his ability to offer us a convincing explanation of the universe, in whole or in part. Lumps
in the metrical oatmeal served up by either do not necessarily
invalidate their enterprise. But if poetry is meant to charm
rather than to instruct, then the poet's technique becomes
much more important, and the notion of poetry's connection
with what we may call, loosely, ideas, becomes a bit suspect.

Such revolutionary notions were being aired in Catullus'
time by the more innovative poets, most prominently perhaps
by the Syrian critic and love poet Philodemus. No doubt one
of the attractions of literary life in Rome for well-bred young
poets like Catullus was the opportunity to rub elbows and
match wits with raffish characters from obscure corners of the
world. Philodemus came from Gadara near the Sea of Galilee,
in those days a center of Hellenistic culture, but now better
known for its swine than for its swain. Somehow Philodemus
managed to find his way to Rome and there became a member
of the circle of L. Calpurnius Piso, in whose villa at Hercula-
neum the carbonized remains of the poet's library were discovered in the eighteenth century.

A polymath and a polemicist who wrote contentiously on
an enormous number of subjects, Philodemus is worth a mo-

ment of our time for his treatise on poetry, the *peri poieimaton*, in which, while disagreeing with everyone else, he almost incidentally propounds his own, surprisingly modern opinions. Philodemus refuses to see poetry as the bearer of lofty ideas and noble sentiments that some of his contemporaries thought it was, nor did he think that the ideas expressed in a poem could be the sole criterion by which we should judge poetry. He argues metaphorically: "Fine ideas are the father of poetry, but words are its mother. It takes after its mother." If poetry is no longer a kind of passive container for elegant ideas, then it must be a marriage of form and content, and the ideas that poetry expresses can no longer be considered without reference to their expression: "There is no good thought, which, if the diction be poor, can make a piece of literature as such, meritorious; nor any content essentially so trivial, that, if the form be good, the contrary effect is not produced."

That being the case, poems on trivial or even absurd subjects—*ineptiae*, as Catullus describes his own poems—ought to be perfectly acceptable, for the poet is now free to write about anything he pleases. If ideas in themselves are less important, so is the question of accurate representation. "Why must true things only be represented," Philodemus asked, "seeing that many false and fabulous things are depicted by the poets most vigorously." As one of Philodemus' critics writes: "According to Neoptolemus, [the] subject matter [of poetry] consisted of real actions and deeds, of facts that existed in the historical, natural, or moral order of things. Philodemus, on the other hand, contended that such a limitation was not justified. *Everything*, he maintained, *could be true in poetry*, including themes fabulous and even false, monsters or legendary spirits, provided they were artistically represented, in concrete and vivid fashion."[15] Although Philodemus does not refer to the poetic imagination as such, it is clear that he understands the existence of such a faculty: everything can be true in poetry.

Many of these ideas seem rather modern, especially the notion that a poem can be written about anything at all, which has underwritten the careers of many of our modernists. Whether or not he agreed with them, these were ideas with which Catullus was familiar. They were ideas that barely survived, as did the poetry of Catullus. It is time to look at his poetry in the context of its survival.

II THE BOOK OF CATULLUS

> This business of survival is far more precarious than the reader may think.
>
> —Yvor Winters

AT PRESENT THE BOOK OF CATULLUS CONSISTS OF 116 POEMS, plus a number of fragments and unfinished drafts of poems, minus three pieces admitted to the canon during the sixteenth century but now generally regarded as spurious; the lacuna left by their passage has been preserved in the numbering of the poems as a part of the history of the text. That history begins with the period in which Catullus wrote his poems, a span of some ten or fifteen years before his death, most likely in the year 54 B.C. During this time or very shortly afterward, his poems found their way into books, and those books—or whatever remained of them—eventually found their way into another book that became, in the absence of competition from any other source, the Book of Catullus, the body of his work as we have it now.

We very nearly did not have it: sometime during the early Middle Ages, books and Book likewise disappeared, went underground; and for the better part of a millennium these poems were a buried presence, a light hidden under a bushel. It has only been for about the last six hundred years that the Book of Catullus has been a text that could be copied and recopied, bringing his work back into circulation.

Catullus tells us more about his habits of composition and about the circumstances in which he worked than any other ancient writer. He is very much like Ernest Hemingway in his self-conscious fascination with the process of his own creativity, as well as in his assurance that his readers will find the subject no less enthralling than he does. In the beginning, he tells us, his poems were jotted down on scraps of used papyrus or on the waxed tablets he carried with him as a kind of notebook. In addition to those poems in which we see Catullus offering to write verses for friends or against enemies, we are also given two very different scenes from the life of a neoteric poet. In poem 50, Catullus describes an afternoon spent in the company of his friend Calvus, drinking wine and playfully collaborating on the improvisation of erotic verses; in poem 68, however, a solitary, sober, and cerebral Catullus regrets that he must decline a friend's request for some poetry, apparently because he does not have at hand the library of Greek authors he uses either as models or for inspiration.

No matter how unbuttoned Catullus wishes to seem, neoteric standards of craftsmanship, as well as the poems themselves, suggest that his idea of poetic composition would ordinarily have entailed a small mountain of palimpsestic papyrus or a waxed tablet worked right down to its wooden backing. Catullus would hardly wish to be seen belaboring trifles—or anything else—in public, but he surely gave his poems a great deal of private attention before he set them loose to find their first audience.

That audience would have learned of them by word of mouth, for the longer ones such as poems 63 and 64 might have been performed in public, either by the poet or by professional actors. The shorter poems would have been recited at banquets, passed on like the good jokes that many of them are, or as exemplary expressions of erotic refinement or deliciously savage wit. Both were important to cultivated Romans, who labored under the perpetual necessity of proving to themselves that they could rival the Greeks in the arts of civilization. In the *Attic Nights* of Aulus Gellius, there is an account of a dinner party that took place about two hundred years after Catullus' death, where he and his friend Calvus are mentioned—by some Greeks, of course—as the only Roman poets able to rival their Hellenic counterparts in the expression of tender feelings in pliant numbers.

But poetry was also a way of lashing out at one's enemies, of making public, and—who knows?—perhaps even terminating their aberrant behavior. One of the recurring motifs in Catullus' poetry is the threat of abuse by iambic verse; in classical times, the iambic meter was the meter of choice for poetic assault. "*At non effugies meos iambos,*" he says in a line from an otherwise lost poem: "But you will not escape from my invective!" A poem could be made out of nothing more substantial than the threat of such an attack. Thus, in poem 40, a certain Ravidus is warned against taking an inappropriate interest in the poet's lover:

> Poor little Ravidus! What madness drives you
> on to be shafted by my sharp iambics?
> What god offended by a faulty prayer
> makes you provoke this quarrel so insanely?
> —Or are you only eager to be noticed,
> a famous man, no matter what the cost is?
> You will be, since you choose to love my darling,
> and for a great while after you'll repent it!   [1–8]

But when innuendo failed to warn off a rival or opponent, only a direct attack could sustain one's credibility, typically, *chez Catulle,* a hair-raising accusation of social impropriety supported by sordid specifics and spelled out in a handful of lines—a scant mouthful of air that wafted its helpless victim up into the dazzling light of publicity. Poem 57 is for Julius Caesar and his lieutenant Mamurra:

> How well these two bad fairies fit together,
> this queenly couple, Caesar and Mamurra!
> —No wonder, for they're like as two like smutches
> (one is from Rome, a Formian the other)
> sunk in too deeply to be gotten rid of:
> a pair of twins with all the same diseases,
> they lie entangled on one couch to scribble,

adulterers both, equally voracious,
sharing nymphetoleptic inclinations:
how well these two bad fairies fit together!   [1–10]

This sort of thing worked, according to the historian Suetonius:
"As [Caesar] himself did not hesitate to say, Catullus inflicted
a lasting stain on his name by the verses about Mamurra. Yet
when he apologized, Caesar invited the poet to dinner that
very same day, and continued his usual friendly relations with
Catullus' father."[1] That anecdote argues both for the poet's
charm and for the politician's shrewd judgment in dealing
with a troublesome satirist.

It also offers us the only view we have of a contemporary
of Catullus responding to his poetry, and since a poet's reputation is usually made by his or her contemporaries, our ignorance of the beginnings of the critical tradition leaves us
much in the dark about such matters as his relations with the
other neoterics, the popularity and circulation of his poems in
and beyond the coterie of his associates, and the nature of the
influence his work had on other neoterics. We may assume
that his poems quickly achieved a reputation for brashness,
sensuality, and elegance among the relatively few people at
Rome for whom such qualities were important. This would
have no doubt led to their first appearance in books, and once
in books the poems would have circulated extensively in their
author's lifetime and for many years afterward.

There was at Rome no Benevolent Society for the Preser-
vation of the Literary Remains of the Neoterics, and so the very
survival of Catullus' poems indicates that someone was looking out for his interests. Yet if the prestige and popularity of
his poems in certain circles worked in some mysterious way
to preserve them for us, other forces not only limited the kind
of influence they would have on subsequent generations but
also made their mere survival problematic. In this regard they
were perhaps their own worst enemies: Romans were not used
to subjectivity in their literature. While it may have been all

very well to create a poetry that would rival the Greeks in delicacy of feeling, the other side of the Romans' cultural inferiority complex was a defensive arrogance: after all, the Greeks were little better than slaves! Many of them, in fact, *were* slaves, writing a slavish, unmanly verse altogether unsuitable for the descendants of Romulus and Remus.

As a result, the shutters of opportunity that Catullus and the neoterics had flung open were quickly closed by those who came after them. In the next generation, Horace and Virgil both had the chance to study Catullus and to learn at first hand from Philodemus, who was still alive when they were young men. It would be inaccurate to say that the younger poets rejected the neoterics entirely, for the concern with craftsmanship and technique they introduced would permanently alter Roman poetry, and the need to reconcile the traditional Roman concepts of civic and martial obligation with the pleasures and refinements of the newly discovered erotic sensibility would become a constant theme: Mars fuming as Venus washes out her nighties in his helmet.

Nevertheless, the age of Augustus demanded a tilting toward Athens and away from Alexandria. Augustus sponsored a return to the old notions of a public poetry that would advance his new agenda: a generation after Catullus' death, the social conditions that had permitted his kind of poetry no longer obtained.

Given the traditional Roman concept of poetry as a didactic instrument, a poet's survival depended in large part on whether he was included in the curriculum: the poetry of Horace and Virgil survived because their values supported the aims of the imperial state. However, a good many of Catullus' poems are enthusiastic celebrations of erotic practices that schoolmasters tend to regard as subversive rather than supportive of public order; our poet would not easily have found his way into the curriculum. Despite the eminent propriety of some of his poems Catullus must have remained a guilty pleasure among the relative few, even up to our own day, when one of his recent editors has seen fit to delete about a third of the poems from his edition on the understandable if contestable grounds that "they do not lend themselves to commentary in English."[2]

During the early years, the poems of Catullus circulated in books that were actually rolls of papyrus like those he describes in poem 22, those

>   good new rolls
> wound up on ivory, with red parchment wrappers,
> lead-ruled, smoothed with pumice   [6–7]

As a means of storing and retrieving information a roll of papyrus leaves much to be desired: aside from the inherent fragility of the material, the rolls were large and cumbersome to hold and read. Even a collection as short as Catullus' would probably have required at least three separate rolls, any one of which might have gotten lost, burned, or, worse, used to wrap mummies in Egypt or mackerel in Padua, the fate Catullus predicts in poem 95 for Volusius' boring *Annales.*

During the third and fourth centuries A.D., the book form we are familiar with today began to supersede the papyrus rolls. The codex, as it was called, was superior to its predecessor in a number of ways; for one, the parchment used in making it was far more durable than papyrus. It was also a good deal more compact: Catullus' poems would now fit easily into a single volume. Its size made the codex more convenient to use and store, factors that would have substantially increased its chances for survival. And the poems of Catullus did find their way, at some time in the late Classical period or early Middle Ages, into at least one codex. If there were others, they have left no trace.

It must have been a descendant of that single volume, containing all of the poems that we now have and in the order in which we now have them, that surfaced in Verona in the year 1300, discovered, it may have been, by Dante's great patron Can Grande della Scala. Its reappearance was commemorated by a certain Benvenuto Campesani in a set of Latin elegiac

verses; it had been found, he said, *sub modio*, under a bushel—
more likely a reference to Matthew 5:15 than to its real hiding
place.

Two copies were made of the *Codex Veronensis*, known as
V, before it disappeared once again. *V* has not since come to
light, and if it were not for those two copies and the copies that
were made of them, only poem 63, preserved independently
in another manuscript, would have escaped oblivion—unless,
of course, that manuscript had also been lost. In that case nothing would have survived of Catullus but his name, a few scraps
of verse, and a reputation for wit and tenderness.

The Book of Catullus was put together by someone who
arranged the poems in three groups, with at least two criteria
always in mind: the length of each poem and the meter in
which it was written. The first group consists of the first sixty
poems, all fairly short and written in various lyric meters, most
frequently the hendecasyllabic (lines of eleven syllables), and
therefore usually referred to as the polymetric poems. The second group consists of eight long poems: poems 61 to 64, in
three different meters (the glyconic, the dactylic hexameter,
and the galliambic, respectively) and poems 65 to 68, all composed in the elegiac meter. The third group, poems 69 to 116,
consists entirely of short poems in the elegiac meter.

That is the Book of Catullus. Whoever put it together ef-
fectively ended the process whose beginnings we are permitted to glimpse in some of the poems themselves: Catullus
improvising verses with his friend Calvus in poem 50 or de-
ploying his irate iambics to demand his wax tablets from the
woman who has stolen them in poem 42. Many of our problems in reading Catullus derive from the fact that, though we
have his poems and we have his Book, we have no clear idea
of the steps that led from one to the other, the process by which
the canon of his work, its reputation and its author's, came
into being. Without that kind of foundation in the quotidian
realities of authorship, criticism is hard-pressed to deal with
many of the most basic questions that arise about an author's

work and reputation: When did he write his poems? Over how many years? In what order? How were they published during his lifetime?

To this last question, there is a partial answer: poem 1, the dedication to his friend Cornelius Nepos, clearly indicates that Catullus prepared at least one book of his own work for publication. Some have argued that poem 1 was meant as a dedication of the entire Book of Catullus as his collected *Poems*. This seems unlikely, for in poem 1 Catullus refers to the collection as a *libellus*, a little book, and he emphasizes the cultural insignificance of its contents. That description fits the polymetric poems quite well, but it hardly does justice to the long poems of the second group, which the poet surely would not have referred to as trifles. In addition, as we will see in chapter VI, poem 1 introduces a theme, the giving of gifts (poetic and otherwise) that Catullus explores in many of the polymetric poems. It seems most likely that the book to Nepos comprised poems from the first group.

There may in fact have been two collections of short poems: A. L. Wheeler cites the poet Martial, who knew a work of Catullus called *Passer*, the sparrow: "Clearly Martial knew some collection of Catullus which began not with the dedication to Nepos that begins our collection but with *Passer deliciae meae puellae* [poem 2] and he was referring . . . to a book . . . beginning with the first sparrow poem."[3] Since poem 1 is a dedicatory poem for one book, Wheeler argues that "we must allow for the possibility that the Sparrow was a second, a different book."[4]

But what relation obtained between the book to Nepos, the *Sparrow* (if it existed) and the Book itself? Did Catullus arrange the poems in their present order, or is the arrangement the work of a later editor who was perhaps unaware of the poet's intentions? Distinguished scholars have lined up on both sides of this issue, supported as often by conviction as by evidence. Ulrich von Wilamowitz-Mollendorff, one of the greatest classicists of the past century, thundered magisterially, "Catullus devoted the most careful thought to the arrangement of his poems: if there is anybody who can't see that, so much the worse for him."[5] In contrast, A. L. Wheeler argued that it was impossible to "reject the arguments of those who . . . have believed that our collection was not made and published by Catullus, but was put together after his death; that in fact its arrangement has greatly obscured the poet's own purposes and methods."[6] Aesthetic order is everywhere apparent to those who believe Catullus responsible for the arrangement of his Book, while those who hold a later editor responsible see little but accident or "planlessness."

The question of whether Catullus was responsible for the arrangement of the poems in the Book is important because one's point of view shapes one's criticism of the poems. If we could be confident that Catullus arranged his work as it now appears in the Book, we could assume that the division of his poems into three groups made aesthetic sense to him, that he thought of the polymetric poems and the poems in elegiac meter as essentially different from each other and from the long poems in several meters. We could also expect that Catullus arranged the poems within each of the three groups in reference to some overarching aesthetic concern, some aim for coherence and unity, and we could be confident that the principles of that arrangement are present in the Book, awaiting our belated discovery. If, however, it could be shown that the arrangement of the Book was the work of a later editor, then critics would be free to ignore the arrangement altogether and pursue other routes through the poems.

Most poets arrange their own poems for publication: they know their own work best and who else would do it for them? If we make the plausible assumption that Catullus resembled most poets in this regard, then it is highly likely that the Catullan order of the original books would persist in some form in the Book, even if the Book had been compiled by a later editor. Assuming the persistence of Catullan order within the text, how would that order be likely to manifest itself? For Catullus, poems were not passive, inert objects neutrally occupying their allotted spaces; rather, they were processes as dynamic and interactive as the people and relationships that inspired them. When the poems got together in books, they were arranged in patterns which revealed the dynamics of their relations with other poems in the collection.

One of Catullus' favorite patterns corresponds to the rhetorical figure *chiasmus*, which arranges elements either diagonally, as in a Greek X:

or by inversion:

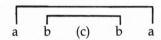

In English verse, two lines from William Butler Yeats' "An Irish Airman Foresees His Death" show the diagonal arrangement:

The years to come seemed waste of breath,

A waste of breath the years behind

while Alexander Pope offers numerous instances of chiastic inversion, as in his "Epistle to a Lady":[7]

A fop *their* *passion* but *their* *prize* **a sot**

We have already seen chiasmus in the poem attacking Caesar and Mamurra, which begins and ends with the same line, a device Catullus uses frequently in the polymetric poems. Catullus is also fond of chiasmus within individual lines of verse, most frequently in poem 64, where one finds numerous lines like this one about the mission of the argonauts:

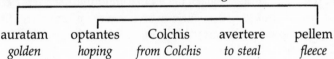

auratam	optantes	Colchis	avertere	pellem
golden	*hoping*	*from Colchis*	*to steal*	*fleece*

Not only lines, but entire poems as well, including—as we shall see in chapter VII—poem 64, his longest, are arranged chiastically.

The chiastic arrangement that Catullus used so often as a structural device in individual poems of all sizes he also used in arranging groups of poems. Poems 61 to 68, the second of the three major groups in the Book of Catullus, have been arranged chiastically:

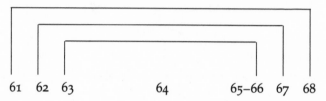

61   62   63   64   65–66   67   68

Each poem in the sequence is related to its opposite number by balance and antithesis of theme, meter, and echoing details. This creates the effect of a single poem in seven parts. A later editor might have had the wit to balance poem 61 (on marriage) with poem 68 (on adultery), but only the poet himself could have written both to serve as mirror reflections of each other. Also, a chiastically arranged sequence is not like one of our open-ended modern poetic sequences: for it to work at all, the poet must put the plan before the poem.

If Catullus arranged poems 61 to 68, then it is highly probable that he also divided the Book into three parts, and it is reasonable to assume that he distinguished between the polymetric poems and the elegiacs in terms of their purposes and possibilities.

It may also be that Catullus arranged the first and third groups of poems himself, but if he did so his principles of arrangement are far from clear; I am inclined to believe that the lucid waters of Catullus' original arrangement of the polymetric poems and the elegiacs have been muddied by a later editor. Nevertheless, it is curious that the first poem in the collection speaks of a gift offered and the last of a gift spurned: that is a truly Catullan touch.

III   LIFE INTO ART

A shilling life will give you all the facts.

—W. H. Auden

ANY NARRATIVE OF THE LIFE OF CATULLUS WOULD BE PROB-
lematic for a number of reasons, the most important of which
is the almost total absence of reliable biographical data. His
contemporaries may have written accounts of his life, as did
the historian Suetonius a century later. These, alas, did not
survive, and as a result some of the most elementary questions
about Catullus remain unanswerable.

But should the facts of his life concern the readers of his
poems? The ritual pieties of our age say no: even as modern
poetry has embraced the revelations of autobiography from
T. S. Eliot to Robert Lowell, modern criticism has sought to
distance itself from the messy contingencies of the lives con-
fessed in the poems. Criticism that focuses on the life rather
than the work now seems quaintly outdated, altogether too
modest for an age in which criticism is often its own subject.
Nevertheless, one of the reasons Catullus seems so modern to
us is his uninhibited use of personal experience as the con-
versational ground for much of his poetry. Many of his poems
are inseparable from those to whom they were written, people
who once walked the streets of Rome just as certainly as he
himself did. The poems are about his relationships with those
people who were, variously, his friends, enemies, lovers, and
rivals; the poems reflect the emotional intensity, variety, and
complexity of these relationships; they are illuminating in
much the same way as fireworks are, but they are far less revealing of the continuities in the life that nurtured them.

A further complication is the fact that Catullus led a life that fairly cries out for the services of a novelist, a cry so far answered most appealingly by Thornton Wilder in his novel *The Ides of March*. Catullus led a life of privilege, pleasure, and romantic brevity, during the years before the crash of the Roman Republic, a period that still resonates for us today. Many of the important figures in his life were such Roman leaders as Julius Caesar, Cicero, Pompey, and the notorious Publius Clodius Pulcher, whose equally notorious sister, Clodia Metelli, is the likeliest model for that complex fiction to which Catullus gave the name of Lesbia.

One would have to be something of a stone, really, not to find such a life interesting, not to want more of it. Here, for example, is A. L. Wheeler: "I would gladly consign to oblivion more than one quarter of his poems if I could gain in exchange a few others containing some information about his ancestry, something more explicit about life in the Verona of his day, something—anything—about his schooldays and youth down to about 61 B.C."[1] It is odd, to say the least, that Catullus can inspire a hunger for biographical information so powerful as to destroy part of the work that inspired it. And yet it seems to me that to read Catullus' poems with any sensitivity is to feel precisely that kind of craving for the facts of his life.

The danger of indulgence lies in yielding to the assumption that the life somehow "explains" the poems. It is indeed difficult to resist believing that if we only knew what urgent message Catullus had to impart to Caecilius, we would "understand" poem 35. Similarly, if we only knew whether the Cato addressed in poem 56 was "that pattern of ancient Roman strictness, M. Porcius Cato" (who would presumably have been both satirized and scandalized by the poem), or the poet's friend Valerius Cato (who might not have been), then we would "understand" the joke behind poem 56—assuming, of course, that there *is* a joke. And so on. The poems seem so clearly taken from life that we assume that whatever we know about the life will clarify them, and in a few cases this is true: without knowing that Lesbia was one of the three sisters of

Publius Clodius Pulcher, we would not be able to make any sense at all of poem 79.

Nevertheless, to read these poems as if they were simply and literally comments on the life lived, or to impose on the poems what we know or think we know about the life, assuming that there is a kind of two-way bridge between life and work to be crossed easily and profitably in both directions, almost always results in a misreading of the poems, which are generally more than mere entries in a poetic autobiography. The poems came out of the poet's life but are not circumscribed by it.

What follows is an attempt to ground the poems in what we know or may reasonably surmise about the poet's life, recognizing that there will come a point when the critic must part company with the biographer and leave the life of the poet to attend to the life of the poems.

His name was Gaius Valerius Catullus, and he was born in Verona in 85 or 84 B.C. and died in Rome thirty years later. His family lived in Verona, a thriving city in Cisalpine Gaul, a Roman province consisting of the part of Gaul that was located in Italy between the Alpine foothills and the river Po. Its inhabitants were known as Transpadanes. Originally settled by Etruscans, the area had been invaded in the fourth century B.C. by Gauls from the north; two centuries later, the Romans turned back another Gallic incursion and established military outposts in the area. After the defeat of Hannibal, Rome secured and developed this northern frontier. During the first century B.C., the province prospered, and Catullus' father was one of its wealthiest and most prominent citizens. Evidence of the family's distinction can be found in the father's friendly relations with Julius Caesar, as well as in the fact that Catullus felt confident enough of his own social position in Rome to write about men like Caesar, Cicero, and Gaius Memmius in terms ranging from familiarly irreverent to downright scathing.

Then as now one of the privileges of great wealth was sur-

face mobility, and Catullus got around. One of his poems refers to a pied-à-terre at Rome and another to a suburban villa
near Tivoli; there was also a family residence in Verona and a
villa at Sirmione, on Lago di Garda, whose half-excavated
ruins are still known locally as *le grotte di Catullo*. These ruins
must once have been an interesting piece of work: dominating
the bluff at the end of the peninsula, they still suggest not only
wealth on an enormous scale but the desire to translate that
wealth into a great work of imaginative and artistic freedom.
It is easy to believe that here was once a place that could have
sheltered the architectonic, mythical vision of poem 64, just as
it is easy to believe that the head of one of the Dioscuri that
was recently found in the ruins could be the image of the god
to whom Catullus offers the model of his yacht in poem 4; and
that the scrap of fresco in the local museum, displaying the
figure of a handsome young man holding a small scroll—
strong mouth, gaiety in the eyes, nut-brown complexion set
against the same blue background as the unclouded sky above
Lago di Garda—could even be a likeness of the poet.

Nothing is known about his education but he tells us that
he became interested in poetry when he was about sixteen,
encouraged by the only relative he mentions in his verse: a
brother whose death, apparently in Asia Minor, probably
around 58 B.C., left him devastated. Catullus would not have
had to leave the province to pursue an education, for the best
of Greek learning was portable, and a number of distinguished
grammatici, teachers of literature and of what we call creative
writing, worked in the province. One of them was the poet
and critic Valerius Cato, an important figure in the neoteric
movement whose renown as a maker of poetic reputations
would have made him a likely person for Catullus to have
sought out as an instructor.

Rome was the intellectual, artistic, and political center of
an empire that still thought of itself as a republic, and Catullus
would have been drawn to the capital by many currents. In
Rome he could continue the education begun in the province

or prove its results by making a name for himself in the literary circles of the capital. And if he had anything to do with the business affairs of his family, he would probably have traveled between the province and Rome on a regular basis.

The poet's familiarity with Caesar and Cicero as well as such important lesser lights as Gaius Memmius and L. Calpurnius Piso must have placed him near the hot center of the political action of his day. His picture of Rome is a fragmentary and idiosyncratic one, vivid and personal glimpses of individuals rather than a systematic exposition of currents and movements, and so it is difficult to determine to what extent public events impinged on his sensibility. During his lifetime, the conspirator Catiline attempted to overthrow the republic from within, and the gladiator Spartacus tried the same from without; Catullus seems to have had no problem in ignoring them both. When he refers to a public event—as in poem 11 when he alludes to Caesar's first invasion of Britain—it is almost always in terms of the event's relevance to his own life.

In Rome or in Verona he met the woman to whom he gave the name with which his own is inseparably linked: Lesbia. Why the pseudonym? Evidence from the poems makes it clear that at some point in their relationship Lesbia was married to another man, and the conventional wisdom holds that the pseudonym was necessary to defend her from the scandal of public knowledge of her adulterous affair with the young poet. Although the conventional wisdom explains why a pseudonym might be used in preference to a real name, it does not explain why a pseudonym should have been used at all, since those were certainly not the only choices open to the poet. Nor is there any reason to believe that Lesbia would have needed to keep secret an intimate friendship with a young man: from what Catullus tells us she was a woman who conducted herself freely, even when her conduct was likely to make her the subject of unsavory gossip. Was Catullus trying to avoid a jealous husband, then? Few Roman marriages were love matches, and among the upper classes they were almost always the result and emblem of alliances between powerful families. In poem 83, Catullus gives us an intriguing glimpse of Lesbia and her mate at home:

> Lesbia hurls abuse at me in front of her husband:
>   that fatuous person finds it highly amusing!
> Nothing gets through to you, jackass—for silence would signal
>   that she'd been cured of me, but her barking and bitching
> show that not only haven't I not been forgotten,
>   but that this burns her: and so she rants and rages.
>
> [1–6]

If Lesbia had been in the habit of discussing her lovers with her husband, she clearly would have neither feared his jealousy nor needed a protective pseudonym. Nor would Catullus have had a reason to keep the affair a secret: even Cicero spoke with indulgence of the need for young men to have their flings, and in several of his poems Catullus makes it clear that in his circle love affairs were only shameful if they were kept secret.

If secrecy was neither necessary nor desirable, then what was the purpose of the pseudonym?

First of all, it would get the attention of the woman who would become Lesbia, would distinguish *this* hopeful suitor from the others who surrounded her. Although the pseudonym became conventional in later Roman erotic poetry, Catullus was apparently the first to have used it, and so its novelty would recommend it as well. The woman who accepted the pseudonym was able to play a role in a script as yet unwritten but most probably a good deal more interesting than the one she was living. The name Lesbia flattered her as a woman sophisticated enough to understand and savor the allusion to Sappho of Lesbos, an allusion that inevitably reminds us of Sappho's erotic relations with women, but this would not have been the primary reference for those of Catullus' contemporaries who gave thought to such matters; for them, Sappho would have been a poetic exponent of erotic refinement in gen-

eral, rather than a specialist in what we—though not she—
would call homosexual relationships.

The pseudonym also served as a way of celebrating the
beloved as an individual in her own right while detaching her
from her former identity. Roman women did not have personal
names as Roman men did: at birth a girl was given one name
only, the feminized version of her father's gentile name, the
name of the *gens* or tribe to which he belonged. If there were
more than one daughter, each received the same name. The
woman who is usually held to be the original of Lesbia was
named Clodia, and she had two sisters, each of whom was also
a Clodia. When the middle Clodia—our Lesbia, most likely—
married one Quintus Metellus Celer, she added his gentile
name to hers and became Clodia Metelli. A woman's name,
then, served as an unfailing reminder that she was totally dependent, first on her father and then on her husband. A
pseudonym would have liberated her at a stroke from that pa-
triarchal domination, giving her a new secret identity shared
only with her lover. How shocking poem 5 must have seemed
to the ears of the moralizing elders, coupling this unprece-
dented use of a pseudonym with the poet's withering contempt for the wisdom of age:

> Lesbia, let us live only for loving,
> and let us value at a single penny
> all the loose flap of senile busybodies!   [1–3]

A mask makes even the most ordinary face a subject of
considerable interest, and so, like the poems in which it prominently appears, the pseudonym draws attention to, rather
than conceals, the affair. The poems Catullus wrote to celebrate his new love would inevitably circulate among the members of his immediate circle, and beyond, for neither he nor
Lesbia would have kept such charming verses to themselves.
Soon everyone who knew them would have known Lesbia's
identity, and before long *everyone* would have known, for that
secret was not meant to be kept.

More like a negligee than a suit of armor, the pseudonym

revealed and flattered in a number of ways the figure it pretended to conceal. To those already in the know, the name revealed its secret metrically: poets after Catullus always chose a false name that was metrically identical to the real one. If Lesbia was indeed Clodia, then the idea came from Catullus: both Lesbia and Clodia consist of a single dactylic foot, one long syllable followed by two short syllables. The reference to Sappho suggests that Lesbia may have been a poet herself, and indeed Cicero speaks of the Clodia usually identified with Lesbia as an experienced poet. No doubt other correspondences existed, for the pseudonym had to conceal and reveal at the same time, but of those two functions revelation is clearly the more important since it guarantees the immortality of the beloved. In the second century A.D., the writer Apuleius cites three poets writing after Catullus—Ticidas, Propertius, and Tibullus—who used pseudonyms for the women they addressed in their erotic poetry, and in each instance he reveals the real name behind the false one.

But who was Lesbia? Apuleius knew her identity and defended his own use of a pseudonym in his love poetry by saying that his accusers might as well charge Catullus with using the name Lesbia for Clodia. From that answer, and from a short poem written in anger by Catullus, it is apparent that Clodia was the sister of a populist demagogue, Publius Clodius Pulcher, a figure known for his political and sexual excesses. Catullus manages to insult him three different ways in just four lines:

> Lesbius is pretty: boy, is he ever! Why Lesbia'd rather
>   have him than you, Catullus, and all your relations!
> Let prettyboy Lesbius sell us all—if he can find even
>   three
>   men of good taste to take his vile kiss when they meet
>   him.   [79, 1–9]

Catullus puns on Clodius' family name in the first phrase of the first line, *Lesbius est pulcher*, first revealing his victim's

name—"Lesbius is (Clodius) Pulcher"—and then playing on
the word's other meaning, "pretty." This leads Catullus into
revealing not only the sister's preference for her brother's bed
but her brother's well-known preference for being the receptive partner in acts of fellatio.

So Lesbia must have been Clodia. But which Clodia?
There were three sisters who carried the feminized version of
their father's gentile name and were all reputedly in love with
their brother. Since the sixteenth century, however, scholars
have generally agreed that Lesbia was Clodia Metelli, the second and most notorious of the three; recent attempts to advance the cause of one or the other of her sisters have so far
failed to make a convincing case.

Clodia Metelli was married to Quintus Metellus Celer, a
prominent though utterly conventional patrician, until his
death in 59 B.C. In 62 B.C., Metellus served as governor of Cisalpine Gaul, where he and Clodia, if she visited or accompanied him, would most likely have met the poet's family and
perhaps even Catullus himself. Or they might have met in
Rome: then as now, in life as in art, it requires very little ingenuity to bring together two interested parties. If Lesbia was
indeed Clodia Metelli, and if she and the poet indeed had an
affair, it would most likely have taken place between 62 and
57 B.C., when the poet left Rome to spend a year traveling in
Bithynia, a province in northwestern Asia Minor, as a member
of the retinue of the provincial governor.

His journey was most likely motivated by his brother's
sudden death while traveling in the east. The brother had been
buried near Troy, and the journey would have afforded Catullus the opportunity to visit the grave and perform the requisite obsequies, the occasion of poem 101:

> Driven across many nations, across many oceans,
>   I am here, my brother, for this final parting,
> to offer at last those gifts which the dead are given
>   and to speak in vain to your unspeaking ashes,
> since bitter fortune forbids you to hear me or answer,

o my wretched brother, so abruptly taken!
But now I must celebrate grief with funeral tributes
    offered the dead in the ancient way of the fathers;
accept these presents, wet with my brotherly tears, and
    now and forever, my brother, hail and farewell.

[1–10]

In poem 68, Catullus, sojourning in Verona, informs a friend
in Rome of his brother's death, and tells of a crisis in his relationship with an unnamed woman who has been rather con-
spicuously unfaithful in his absence. A journey to the east at
this time might have had the secondary advantage of allowing
Catullus to escape from an erotic entanglement that had become not only a private torment but a public embarrassment.

The one major event in Catullus' life that can be dated
with any precision from the poems is the year he spent in
Bithynia: Catullus identifies the governor he accompanied as
Gaius Memmius, who had served as *praetor*, one of the con-
sular magistrates at Rome, in 58 B.C. Ordinarily, praetors were
responsible for a year of foreign service immediately after serving in Rome, and so Memmius and his entourage (which included another poet, Catullus' friend Gaius Helvius Cinna)
would have been in Bithynia from the spring of 57 to the spring
of 56 B.C.

Memmius must have known Catullus before inviting him
to Bithynia: Memmius was a literary man, a writer of poetry
and the person to whom Lucretius dedicated *De Rerum Natura*.
No doubt Memmius chose Catullus as a traveling companion
for his poetic rather than his administrative talents.

Catullus may have had reasons for traveling east besides
fraternal piety and the desire to end a problematic love affair:
several poems written after his journey depict him somewhat
less piously as a young man on the make. Spending a year in
colonial administration was common for young men of Catullus' class, and the reasons for so doing were hardly obscure:
as E. T. Merrill put it, "The ordinary motive was not only a

love of adventure, but the desire for acquiring wealth at the expense of the provincials in one of the dozen ways possible under a friendly and not too conscientious official patron."[2] If those were his expectations, he claims to have been disappointed, for after his tour of duty, Catullus returned to Rome out of pocket and out of sorts with Memmius, whom he seems to have held responsible for this unhappy turn of events.

He may have written poetry while he was away from Rome: the elegy for his brother purports to have been composed on the site of his grave, and the remarkable narrative in poem 63 of a young man's emasculating passion for the goddess Cybele is set in the northwestern part of Asia Minor, an area Catullus probably visited during his year abroad. Nevertheless, to paraphrase Dr. Johnson, it appears that the finest prospect the province offered was that of leaving it, for there are a number of exultant poems of homecoming: a joyous celebration of his impending departure, two lyrical celebrations of his return to Italy, poems delighting in the return of his friends Veranius and Fabullus from their journeys, and several comical reminiscences of his financially disappointing venture into colonial administration.

Was Clodia Lesbia? In the past, this speculation was too often used naïvely to construct a love affair as chronologically and geographically precise as a railway timetable; the reconstituted love affair was then used to explain the poems. Catullus apparently had a relationship with a woman whom he called Lesbia, and Lesbia was probably Clodia Metelli, but there is no way we can say that Catullus had an affair with Clodia. We would not even have *his* word for it, since he says nothing about anyone named Clodia. He tells us only about Lesbia, and the pseudonym inevitably creates a paradoxical pair of equations: *Lesbia is Clodia*, and, at the same time and with equal truth, *Lesbia is not Clodia*. As ordinarily curious human beings, we cannot help but become involved to some extent in the first equation; nevertheless, the task of criticism is to explore the possibilities contained in the second. To do this, one must consider Lesbia not as a real person possessed of certain traits and qualities but as a theme running through many of Catullus' poems, an emblem abstracted and idealized from the poet's experience, the projection of his erotic expectations and disappointments.

In the Book of Catullus, four different kinds of poems develop the theme of Lesbia. The first is a poem of courtship in which Catullus offers himself as a potential lover and attempts to persuade Lesbia to accept him. A second kind of poem attempts to mythologize Lesbia's refusal to commit herself to him entirely. In a third kind of poem, closely related to the second, he self-consciously analyzes their relationship, focusing on the effect her infidelities have had on it and on him. Finally, there are some poems in which he attempts to dismiss her, sometimes tentatively, sometimes brutally.

It is difficult to read these poems without arranging them in a more or less chronological scenario of a reasonably probable love affair, beginning in ardor and ending in odium. Such an arrangement may be too neat: poems referring to a period of mutual bliss, as well as poems alluding to a reconciliation, suggest that the relationship might have been more cyclical than linear.

In the first three of its four stanzas, Catullus' poem 51 imitates an ode of Sappho's in which she describes her passion for a woman whom she sees sitting with a man who appears to be either a lover or a suitor. Poem 51 may have been the first Catullus actually wrote to Lesbia, and it is certainly the one in which he creates her and defines their situation by allusion to Sappho:

> To me that man seems like a god in heaven,
> seems—may I say it? greater than all gods are,
> who sits by you and without interruption
>   watches you, listens
> to your light laughter, which casts such confusion
> onto my senses, Lesbia, that when I

gaze at you merely, all of my well-chosen
    words are forgotten
as my tongue thickens and a subtle fire
runs through my body while my ears are deafened
by their own ringing and at once my eyes are
    covered in darkness   [1–2]

She is clearly the self-possessed *domina*, the commanding mistress, and he is her worshipful slave, silenced in her presence, unstrung by the intensity of his desire for her. And in the triangle of Lesbia, the unnamed suitor at her side, and the poet enviously observing them from a distance, we have the essential leitmotif of the Lesbia poems: the poet's possession of his beloved is always threatened or thwarted by her involvement with (and preference for) another man or other men.

From this compact seed comes a closely knit, tightly argued courtship sequence composed of poems 2, 3, 5, and 7. The romantic idealization of Lesbia by allusion to Sappho, the theme of the poet's helplessness in love, and the presence of another man in Lesbia's life are all developed further in poem 2:

Sparrow, you darling pet of my beloved,
which she caresses, presses to her body
or teases with the tip of one sly finger
until you peck at it in tiny outrage!
—For there are times when my desired, shining
lady is moved to turn to you for comfort,
to find (as I imagine) ease for ardor,
solace, a little respite from her sorrow—
if only I could play with you as she does,
and be relieved of my tormenting passion.   [1–10]

Lesbia is distracting herself from the sorrows of love by playing with her pet sparrow. Lesbia's sparrow has received a good deal of critical and even ornithological attention over the years, but the cause of her mysterious sorrow has been generally ignored. It is clearly brought on by love—but love for whom? For

Catullus? Not likely: he gracefully confesses his feelings for her in the poem's last line, and since he *is* in love with her, why would she be so unhappy if she were in love with him? Surely love requited should be a source of comfort to them both. The only possibility that fits the facts of the poem is that the poet's beloved is in love with someone else, someone for whom she suffers in the same way that Catullus suffers for her. Poem 2 thus reconfigures the triangle of poem 51.

Lesbia was undoubtedly aware that poem 51 was an imitation of Sappho; no doubt she would have caught the allusion in poem 2 to another poem of Sappho's, an ode in which the poet calls upon Aphrodite to aid her in a case of unrequited love. Sappho beseeches the goddess to fly down to her as she did once before in her chariot drawn by a team of *strouthoi*, sparrows—birds that, because of their reputed wantonness, were held sacred by the goddess. "Whom am I to persuade this time to lead you back to her love?" Aphrodite asks.[3] Like Sappho's poem, poem 2 is also about persuasion, serving as a courtship present, a charm sent to entice the reluctant beloved.

Poem 2 also plays a role in the sequence of which it is a part. It divides evenly in two: the first five lines offer a light-hearted description of the poet's lady idling away the time with her pet, while the last five lines reveal the sorrows of the poet and his beloved. Those sorrows are the shadow of death that is always stalking us, and, as developed at the beginning of poem 3, advance the poet's argument a notch by stating the first term of what will become a kind of poetic syllogism: sparrows die:

> Cry out lamenting, Venuses and Cupids,
> and all below endowed with their refinement:
> the sparrow of my lady lives no longer!
> Sparrow, the darling pet of my beloved,
> that was more precious to her than her eyes were;
> it was her little honey, and it knew her
> as well as any girl knows her own mother;

it would not ever leave my lady's bosom
but leapt up, fluttering from yon to hither,
chirrupping always only to its mistress.
It now flits off on its way, goes, gloom-laden
down to where—word is—there is no returning.
Damn you, damned shades of Orcus that devour
all mortal loveliness, for such a lovely
sparrow it was you've stolen from my keeping!
O hideous deed! O poor little sparrow!
It's your great fault that my lady goes weeping,
reddening, ruining her eyes from sorrow!   [1–18]

Even sparrows, especially dear to the goddess of love, and
even this one, especially dear to the poet's beloved, even he
must die. The second term of the syllogism becomes clear
when we realize that Orcus devours all mortal loveliness, not
only sparrows but their mistresses as well. Lesbia is a sparrow;
it is Lesbia she mourns for.

Were this a logical syllogism, its conclusion would be obvious: Lesbia must die, as all of us poor sparrows must. And
that conclusion appears in poem 5: "night is one sleep from
which we never waken." But the conclusion to the logical syllogism we expect is overwhelmed by the conclusion to the poetic syllogism. This is a syllogism of pure intentionality, which
refuses to surrender to death, and begins in fact with a triumphant resurrection from the world of Orcus, a summons back
to life with the word that in Latin means "Let us live," *Vivamus!* Since we cannot avoid that unending sleep, we must fling
ourselves on the mercies of the moment:

Lesbia, let us live only for loving,
and let us value at a single penny
all the loose flap of senile busybodies!
Suns when they set are capable of rising,
but at the setting of our own brief light
night is one sleep from which we never waken.
Give me a thousand kisses, then a hundred,
another thousand next, another hundred,

a thousand without pause and then a hundred
until when we have run up our thousands
we will cry "Bankrupt!" hiding our assets
from ourselves and any who would harm us,
knowing the volume of our trade in kisses.   [1–13]

Poem 5 presents a vision of total erotic liberation and absorption that would inevitably exclude not just Lesbia's other lovers but the moral demands of society as represented by the senile busybodies, the gossiping elders. What Catullus wants is nothing less than sole and exclusive possession—given all of those thousands of kisses, when would she have time for anyone else? No doubt Lesbia viewed the prospect differently than her lover, and in the first line of poem 7 we can detect a note of world—or poet—weariness in the echo of her response:

My Lesbia, you ask how many kisses
would be enough to satisfy, to sate me!
—As many as the sandgrains in the desert
near Cyrene, where Silphium is gathered,
between the shrine of Jupiter the sultry
and the venerable sepulcher of Battus!
—As many as the stars in the tacit night
that watch as furtive lovers lie embracing:
only to kiss you with that many kisses
would satisfy, could sate your mad Catullus!
A sum to thwart the reckoning of gossips
and baffle the spell-casting tongues of envy!   [1–12]

A display of neoteric wit and erudition, poem 7 is the most elaborate of the poems of courtship.

It seems possible that these charms worked, that there was a period in their relationship when Catullus had reason to believe he was Lesbia's only lover, and he even seems to have believed she intended to marry him. In other poems Catullus looks back to a period of idyllic singlemindedness when what he wanted, as he says in poem 8, was what she also wanted. The poems do not indicate how long this stage of ec-static hopefulness persisted, but it appears to have been in-terrupted when the death of his brother called the poet back to Verona and he began to receive reports of Lesbia's infidel-ities.

The poet's creation and celebration of Lesbia as an ideal of erotic liberation would inevitably have conflicted with his need to possess and be possessed by her, as well as with her apparent need to remain independent. In several important poems, Catullus demonstrates one way of handling the irrec-oncilable differences between them by mythologizing their re-lationship and projecting its drama onto a larger screen than the lyric can provide, thus transforming his passion and her infidelities into something beyond the reach of praise or blame.

The mythologizing of their relationship is shown as it de-velops in poem 68, beginning with a request from a friend in Rome for some poetry that will console him in the absence of his mistress. Catullus explains that because the recent death of his brother has brought him back to Verona he is unable to comply: the many volumes of Greek poetry he keeps in Rome, either as models or for inspiration, did not accompany him north. The poem almost ends on that unpromising note, but immediately starts up again with Catullus bursting into an ex-postulation to the Muses:

> Muses, I can't remain silent concerning the matter
>   in which I was so greatly aided by Allius,
> or Time as it rushes on through the oblivious ages
>   will cover up that zeal of his in the night's blindness
> [41–44]

As of course it did. But what was the aid that Allius offered? Catullus goes on to explain:

> He gave me access, a path to a field once forbidden,
>   he gave me a house and gave me its mistress also,
> and in that place we explored our mutual passion.

> There my radiant goddess appeared to me, stepping
> lightly and paused to stand with the sole of her sandal
>   on the well-worn threshold as her bright foot crossed
>   it   [67–72]

This recollection of the lovers' mutual passion reveals that the
idealization of Lesbia has advanced beyond the literary arche-
type: she is now his radiant goddess. Her being and her acts
are to be considered under the aspect of eternity, as though
she were one of the immortals, but the immortal with whom
Catullus chooses to compare her later in the poem comes as
something of a shock:

> My darling lacked little or nothing of that perfection
>   when she brought herself to lie in my embraces,
> for Cupid was there and constantly flitted about her,
>   the god resplendent in his bright saffron tunic!
> So, if she must have others besides her Catullus, we'll
>   suffer
>   the infrequent lapses of our artful lady,
> lest we should too much resemble respectable people:
>   often Juno herself, the greatest of goddesses,
> gulps back her passionate rage at the sins of her
>   husband,
>   knowing the countless tricks of promiscuous Jove!
>   [131–140]

Lesbia is Jove the philanderer, and Catullus plays long-
suffering Juno, biting back her anger at his infidelities. In
poem 51, his desire left him speechless, incapable of acting;
here, he admits, his anger at her infidelities reduces him to a
similar state, though a more drastic one, for her behavior
changes him into a speechless woman.

Another transformation takes us into areas of experience
darkened by the blood of sacrifice. In poem 63, we find the
same unequal contest between the domina and her helpless
slave raised to the level of ritual. The passion of a young man
named Attis for the goddess Cybele drives him into a frenzy

in which he leaves home, family, and friends, rushing off to
Phrygia—home of the cult of the goddess—where he castrates
himself and leads a throng of her devotees through the forest
in a worshipful rout. When he comes to his senses the next
day, Attis cries out in horror over his self-mutilation and attempts to flee from the dominion of the goddess, but when she
hears him she sends one of her lions to drive him back into the
forest.

The sensible Romans believed that a man who could not
control his passions lacked virility. The transformation of
Love's Slave into a speechless woman that occurs in poem 68
is here more radically presented as an act of castration, all the
more horrifying because it is self-inflicted. The implacable and
ferocious domina wills both the emasculation of her slave and
his exile in the forest, an endless separation from the rational
and supportive society he willingly abandoned to join her service. Attis may lead the rout of her worshippers but he receives
no special status, and having now made the same essential
sacrifice all her other followers made, there is no turning back.

In poem 63, the theme of Lesbia is explored as the myth
of Cybele, and it seems likely that the tableaus in poem 64 of
Theseus' abandonment of Ariadne on Dia and her tearful complaint against his betrayal represent yet another treatment of
the theme, casting Ariadne as Catullus and Theseus as Lesbia.
The thematic cross-dressing is similar to that in poem 68 where
Catullus becomes Juno and Jove Lesbia. Ariadne's complaint
ends in a prayer to Jove, a cry for revenge against Theseus,
and as we will see, poem 76 ends in a prayer to the gods in
which Catullus beseeches them to end the long sickness of his
love affair.

The mythologizing of Lesbia continues the process of idealization begun in the poems romanticizing her under the sign
of the Sapphic Muse. That mythologizing dramatizes their relationship, but Catullus does not neglect to examine it in a
rational way. In poem 68, he combines these processes, mythologizing their relationship and stepping back to examine his
need for her and her need for others. He reveals the process

of rationalizing his attachment to her more explicitly in the continuation of the passage I quoted above:

> But it's indecent, comparing men with immortals;
> . . . .
> . . . .
>   you'll get no thanks for playing the bothersome
>   parent.
> Nor was she brought to me on the right hand of her
>   father,
>   out of a house made fragrant with Syrian incense,
> but in the marvelous nighttime she came with those
>   precious
>   gifts stolen right out of the lap of her husband!
> So it is really enough if she saves for us only those days
>   she marks with the white stone of celebration
>
>   [141–148]

Since she is one of the immortals and their relationship began in adultery, he will settle for having her on a part-time basis—the white stones marked special holidays. Was he serious? Perhaps. Although he appears to accept the situation, the failure of their relationship to satisfy his expectations leads to great emotional turmoil, and to poems in which he examines his emotional life minutely and unsentimentally, never with greater intensity and compression than in poem 85:

> I hate and love. And if you should ask how I can do
>   both,
>   I couldn't say; but I feel it, and it shivers me.   [1–2]

Her need for men besides Catullus does not change, and other elegiac epigrams explore the effect her inability or unwillingness to commit herself has had on him:

> To such a state have I been brought by your mischief,
>   my Lesbia,
>   and so completely ruined by my devotion,

> that I couldn't think kindly of you if you did the best
>   only,
>   nor cease to love, even if you should do—everything!
>   [75, 1–4]

The poet's ability to say "I hate and I love" represents his recognition of the inherent paradox of his passion: a romantic love for his own creation, an ideal of liberating and liberated sexuality, yoked to the demands made on a real woman for exclusivity and total possession, demands which—after she resisted them—turned a keen lover into a keener enemy. He was able to sustain that ambivalent balance between love and hate for only so long, until the scales tilted and we find that the poems analytically examining emotion and behavior give way to poems of violent rage and public excoriation in which he brutalizes Lesbia's name and reputation.

The poet could salvage his pride only by dishing out rough justice, holding Lesbia and her multiple lovers up to scorn in the court of public opinion, as he does in poem 37, where she is the center of lascivious attention in a low dive whose trade only *think* they're rough. Catullus will show them all:

> Bawdyhouse barroom, nine pillars past the temple
> of Castor and Pollux! And you who get drunk there!
> —Can you believe that you're the world's only lovers,
> the only ones licensed to offer the ladies
> a proper screwing? The rest of us are just goats?
> You hundred dullards, sitting in a row! Or is it
> two hundred, dullards? Do you think that I wouldn't
> dare to fuck over the lot of you as you sit there?
> Think what you want to, dullards—but I'll scribble
> cocks and cunts all over the front of your building!
>   [1–10]

Here she presides and here her lovers attend her, not just the beautiful people but *omnes pusilli et semitarii moechi*, all of her common crew of cocksmen and lechers. Today's favorite, one

Egnatius, a Spaniard, is also attacked, hilariously, in poem 39,
for his ever-present grin and homemade mouthwash.

In poem 51, Catullus created Lesbia; in poem 11 (datable
from internal reference to either 55 or 54 B.C. after the poet's
return from Bithynia) Catullus destroys her, once more using
the Sapphic meter:

> Aurelius and Furius, true comrades,
> whether Catullus penetrates to where in
> outermost India booms the eastern ocean's
>   wonderful thunder;
>
> whether he stops with Arabs or Hyrcani;
> Parthian bowmen or nomadic Sagae;
> or goes to Egypt, which the Nile so richly
>   dyes, overflowing;
>
> even if he should scale the lofty Alps, or
> summon to mind the mightiness of Caesar
> viewing the Gallic Rhine, the dreadful Britons
>   at the world's far end—
>
> you're both prepared to share all these adventures
> and any others which the gods may send me.
> Back to my girl then, carry her this bitter
>   message, these spare words:
>
> May she have joy and profit from her cocksmen,
> go down embracing hundreds all together,
> never with love but without interruption
>   wringing their balls dry;
>
> nor look to my affection as she used to,
> for she has left it broken, like a flower
> at the edge of a field, after the plowshare
>   brushes it, passing.   [1–24]

Instead of a single lover, godlike in his privilege, with which
the myth began, a host of lechers now attends Lesbia. In the
depths of its feeling, poem 11 is closer to poem 63 than to poem
51. At the end, Lesbia is a profane version of the goddess; like

Cybele, she also mutilates the genitalia of her worshippers, the undiscriminating lechers who attend her in the disreputable bar of poem 37. The male-female reversal of the last stanza transforms Lesbia into the phallic plowshare and the poet into the broken flower. In both poems, the attempt to break away from the domina is set in the context of a journey: the frenzied wanderings of Attis parallel the imagined wandering of Catullus from the eastern ocean to the western sea. Attis also attempts to reach the ocean but is driven back by one of Cybele's lions, rude phallic energy shearing its way through the greenery:

> Unyoked, that monster arouses himself, and when he is
>   maddened
> he rushes off, gouges a jagged path through the thickets
> until he comes to the watery edge of the gleaming
>   seacoast
> and sees delicate Attis there by the marmoreal waters:
> he bears down upon him. Possessed, Attis flees back to
>   that wild forest
> in which he spent all the rest of his life as Cybele's
>   handmaid.   [63, 85–90]

Catullus is rarely obscure: the question his readers are likely to ask is not "What does this mean?" but "How does he mean this?" Or "Does he *really* mean this?" Consider the opening lines of poem 16:

> Pedicabo ego vos et irrumabo,
> Aureli pathice et cinaede Furi

This is certainly an unusual way to begin a poem. The poet is threatening two characters named Furius and Aurelius with a different kind of homosexual rape for each of them according to preference. The verbs *pedicare* and *irrumare* specify the acts and orifices involved and the terms *pathicus* and *cinaedus* likewise label the preferred sexual activities of Furius and Aurelius. Sexually receptive males were so labeled by their preference for oral or anal intercourse. I offer a prose paraphrase, far from adequate in its brio, but sufficiently explicit: "I will rape the pair of you as each of you prefers it: you rectally, anal-receptive Furius, and you orally, oral-receptive Aurelius." The English language provides the groaning translator with no exact equivalent for most of the terms Catullus uses, and even if it did, our ways of sexual stereotyping differ from his: our culture labels people by gender preference as heterosexual or homosexual. The exclusivity of these terms would not have been understood in the Rome of Julius Caesar, where bisexual activities were taken for granted and where men labeled one another according to whether one was the inseminator or the inseminated in any sexual union. Insemination in the defense of virility was held to be no vice: Catullus is actually proving his manhood here by threatening to rape his enemies and their submission—they don't reply, do they?—demonstrates their effeminacy and passivity.

Does he really mean it? If we take that question seriously, we will find ourselves wondering about the poet's relationship to Furius and Aurelius, who make their occasional appearances in his poems in a variety of roles and with an absence of continuity and motivation that would no doubt remind Lady Bracknell of the worst excesses of the modern French novel. What were they to him? It is tempting to feel that if we could answer that question we would "understand" this poem and the others in which Furius and Aurelius are addressed or discussed. But the poem resists being understood in so simple a way.

Does he really mean it? It is not always easy to say.

Poems 41 and 43, for instance, are commonly held to have been written before the end of the affair with Lesbia. In poem 41, Catullus appears to be indirectly assaulting one of his favorite villains, Caesar's lieutenant Mamurra, by proclaiming his astonishment that Mamurra's mistress Ameana has set the price of her favors so far above their worth:

Ameana puella defututa
tota milia me decem poposcit,

ista turpiculo puella naso,
decoctoris amica Formiani.
propinqui, quibus est puella curae,
amicos medicosque convocate:
non est sana puella, nec rogare
qualis sit solet aes imaginosum.

This girl (I mean fucked-over Ameana)
demands ten thousand from me altogether!
—That girl whose nose is utterly repulsive,
whore of that bankrupt wastrel from Formiae!
Now you—the girl's relations—you're in charge here,
you'd better call her friends and get the doctors:
she's out of her mind, this girl—and never bothers
to pause before a mirror for reflection.   [1–8]

In poem 43, he returns to the subject of Ameana without nam-
ing her, expressing his astonishment that people in the province now compare her to his Lesbia:

Salve, nec minimo puella naso
nec bello pede nec nigris ocellis
nec longis digitis nec ore sicco
nec sane nimis elegante lingua,
decoctoris amica Formiani.
ten provincia narrat esse bellam?
tecum Lesbia nostra comparatur?
o saeclum insapiens et infacetum!

Greetings to you, girl of the nose not tiny,
the feet not pretty, eyes not darkly shadowed,
stubby fat fingers, mouth forever spraying
language that shows us your lack of refinement,
whore of that bankrupt wastrel from Formiae!
Is it your beauty they praise in the province?
Do they compare you to our Lesbia?
Mindless, this age. And insensitive, really!   [1–8]

This is usually taken as a graceful little compliment to Lesbia.
Is it? I find such a reading more than a bit suspect: one of the

curious things about the polymetric poems is that, with the
exception of those in which he is courting Lesbia (poems 2, 3,
5, 7, and 51), all of the rest of the poems in the first sixty that
are either to her or about her are poems in which he is bru-
talizing her reputation. And so from poem 7 to poem 51, there
are only these two in which Catullus has anything nice to say
about Lesbia, if these are in fact complimentary.

And if they are compliments, they are rather strange ones.
Poem 41 cannot be anything but a trashing of the reputation
of this Ameana: she is a golddigger, the consort of a swindler;
she is not only physically unattractive, but insensitive to the
fact; the repetition of *puella* throughout the poem (and especially the phrase *puella defututa*) suggests that although she still
pretends to be young and desirable the world has for too long
had its way with her. And of course she is also described as
insane. In the second poem Catullus itemizes her unattractive
traits. "And you know what they're saying about this slut in
the province, darling? They're saying that she resembles *you!*"
If people were for whatever reason comparing Lesbia and
Ameana, wouldn't Lesbia want to keep it quiet? And why
would the people of the province—that is, Verona and envi-
rons—compare Lesbia and Ameana?

To answer these questions, we would probably have to
know why Catullus so hated Mamurra. Catullus attacks the
man under his own name and under the obscene pseudonym
Mentula (slang for penis) in eight poems, one more than he
devotes to the loathsome Gellius. Why? Scholars seem re-
markably incurious about Catullus' hatred of the man. In most
of the poems he is attacked for his rapacity: he is a wastrel,
getting and spending at an indecent rate. But, like the word
indecent, getting and spending also have their sexual conno-
tations, and in most of the poems against Mamurra an element
of envy or sexual jealousy is present as well. Caesar's hench-
man is attacked in poem 29 for his extravagant ways with other
people's money, but what really seems to rile Catullus is the
way in which ready coin has given him another kind of instant
access:

—Popping with pride now, he struts off, promenading
through all the best bedrooms like a new Adonis,
or a snowy dove cock, Aphrodite's darling!   [6–8]

Could Mamurra have been a rival of his? But for whom? Poem
43 names Lesbia: Could people have been talking about Lesbia
and Ameana in the same breath because both of them were
sleeping with Mamurra?

That is one possibility. But how does Ameana, mentioned
in poem 41, fit into the scenario? Not very well, as it happens:
Ameana has been something of a problem ever since the mysterious *V* came out from under its bushel. The word appears
in the earliest manuscripts as *a me an a*, the spacing perhaps
indicative of scribal uncertainty: a word or phrase that had
been there before was now missing. A name, either that of a
person or the place that she came from, seemed necessary;
however, Ameana wasn't a name had by anyone else or found
anywhere else, and scholars tried to provide Mamurra's mistress with a more plausible name: Arretina? Ametina? An-
niana?

One fascinating possibility is that Ameana was not a person at all but an accident of transmission. In the nineteenth
century, a commentator suggested reading *amens illa* for
Ameana: "That demented *puella defututa*." Though this reading found no favor with later editors, internal evidence supports it: as the poem begins, the poet calls attention to the
woman's madness and then returns to that idea, developing it
in the last four lines: "Did I say crazy? I mean, this one should
be committed, right away."

It is also easy to see how *amens illa* could have become
Ameana: all that would have been needed was the obliteration
of a few letters in the phrase *ame*[ns i]*lla*, and a scribe's wrong
guess about whether the next two characters made up a single
n or two *l*'s. He decided on *a me na* but knew the meter demanded another syllable and the likeliest possibility must have
seemed *ame a na*. Thus Mamurra's deliberately anonymous
mistress acquired her improbable name.

Now, if there were no Ameana, then Mamurra's mistress could only have been the woman who was Lesbia, and these two poems could then be read as belonging to that group of polymetric poems in which Catullus brutalizes Lesbia's reputation, nowhere more cleverly than here. When he loved her he thought her a great beauty, but those days are gone, and now that she is Mamurra's mistress, Catullus, disgusted by her moral ugliness, cattily details the defects of her appearance and manners before identifying her with a single line: *tecum Lesbia nostra comparatur?* Do they compare you with our Lesbia? They do, since she is. Catullus uses the same phrase *Lesbia nostra* in poem 58 where he complains to Caelius about the utter degradation of his former mistress.

My interest here is not in arguing for this reading of the two poems over the traditional reading—though I do find it a good deal more plausible—but in suggesting that what we know or think we know about the lives may interfere with our understanding of the poems. The critic who argues that the Rufus who suffers from underarm goat odor in poem 69 or the fellow in poem 71 suffering from gout could not possibly have been Caelius Rufus because it is known that Caelius Rufus was an elegant man and an excellent dancer to boot is missing the point of these poems by a country mile. Their hallmarks are reticence, irony, and playfulness; they argue, as Catullus' contemporary Philodemus did, that anything can be true in poetry. To understand the kind of commitments they make and the kind they are incapable of making, we must learn to school ourselves in their playfulness.

II   POETIC LICENSE

IV OF POETRY
AND PLAYFULNESS

The poem is at last between two persons instead of two pages.

—Frank O'Hara

THE FIGURE OF THE MODERN POET AS AN INDIVIDUAL ALIENATED from society is by now one of the clichés of our time and culture: "I mate with my free kind upon the crags," Ezra Pound yelped exultantly.[1] But his friend Yeats saw the process that led up to such a declaration with a more jaundiced eye and accorded the moderns a somewhat lower place in "Three Movements":

> Shakespearean fish swam the sea, far away from land;
> Romantic fish swam in nets coming to the hand;
> What are all those fish that lie gasping on the strand?[2]

The solipsistic nature of much contemporary poetry has become something of a scandal in certain quarters, or quarterlies, but there is nothing new about it. "Divorce is the sign of knowledge in our times," said William Carlos Williams;[3] the occasions of modern poetry are occasions in which the poet stands apart from the community. Solitude yields poetry: social occasions yield verse. Should the poor fish that lies gasping on the strand discover a perfect nautilus shell, that would be something to write a poem about; but the celebration of two friends' silver wedding anniversary is merely an occasion for verse. In our time such occasional verse has become so commercialized that when you care enough to send, if not write, the very best, you can always rely on the anonymous wordsmiths of greeting card companies.

In our culture, the interaction between writer and reader

during the creative process is sharply limited by our understanding of the autonomy of the artist and the integrity of the
poem. Solitary poets produce poems to be read by isolated
readers; when poet and audience meet at a poetry reading, the
event more commonly resembles a communion service than a
dinner party. Indeed, the notion that an audience would have
any say about what kind of poems the poet should write or
how they should be written strikes us as absurd. The poet who
goes on leaping from crag to crag in search of his own kind,
shaking off those who cannot keep up with him, is still an ad-
mired figure in our time, at least in academe.

But poetry was a profoundly social art for Catullus and
his circle, and the poet who wandered the strand in search of
inspiration would have been regarded as wasting his time. For
Catullus, poetry was made out of one's relationships with
friends, lovers, and enemies. Its reception was also social:
poems were recited at dinner parties and criticized there as
well. And so, before Catullus' poems found a general audience
they were exposed to a coterie of intimates to praise or find
fault with them. This situation made Catullus responsive to
the needs and wishes of the few but fit, an accommodation we
are likely to find confusing, given the alienation of so much
artistic activity in our time. This awareness on Catullus' part
makes his poetics more accepting of conventions than ours,
more willing to establish shared space between reader and
writer, like a blanket spread between them for a picnic.

For Catullus, a poem was both an object to achieve and
part of a continuing process, a dialogue between writer and
reader, or—as in poem 50—between poet and poet. The art of
composing such poetry was serious and demanding. The adjective applied to Catullus by Ovid, Propertius, and Horace
was *doctus*: the *doctus poeta* not only possessed a scholarly
knowledge of the poetic tradition and the formal requirements
of his art but also composed verse with the expertise of a vir-
tuoso. And yet, coexisting with this high seriousness was an

equally compelling notion of poetry as play. In poem 50, Catullus reminds his friend Calvus of how

> Just yesterday, Licinius, at leisure
> we played around for hours with my tablets
> writing erotic verse as we'd agreed to,
> each of us taking turns at improvising
> line after line in meter after meter,
> adjuncts to wine and witty conversation.   [1–6]

Some critics have assumed that Catullus is here describing nothing more than a parlor game between two poets. But while there is playfulness in these lines there is seriousness as well. The first three lines of the poem might almost be a neoteric manifesto, a red flag waved in the faces of the censorious elders such as Cicero, for whom the notion of a day stolen from the active life and given over wholly to joining a friend in the composition of erotic verse in a spirit of mutual naughtiness would have been a serious provocation indeed. Nothing in these lines suggests that the poetry produced during this session was any "lighter" than the verse Catullus usually wrote, and if the method of composition seems strange to us, the fault may lie in our provinciality. Once again, our high regard for the individuality and autonomy of the poet can blind us to the value of poetic composition considered as a conversation between equals and prevent us from taking seriously poems composed in a playful manner. Japanese poets would no doubt see a resemblance between what Calvus and Catullus were doing and the way they themselves sat down and composed those intricately constructed collaborative poems called *renga*. Clearly the act of composition affected Catullus profoundly:

> And when I left you, I was so on fire
> with all your brilliant and ironic humor
> that after dinner I was still excited,
> and sleep refused to touch my eyes with quiet.

> In bed and totally unstrung by passion,
> tossing in agony, I prayed for sunrise,
> when I could be with you in conversation.   [7–13]

The two poets had spent their day writing erotic poetry, and erotic poetry has a very specific aim: to quote Frank O'Hara again, "As for measure and other technical apparatus, that's just common sense: if you're going to buy a pair of pants you want them to be tight enough so everyone will want to go to bed with you."[4] Catullus likewise, if not even more so. Calvus and Catullus were writing poetic charms to compel desire in others, and when Catullus describes the effect that composing the stuff with Calvus has had on him, he resorts to the stock description of Greek and Latin epigrams—the thwarted lover tossing and turning on his sleepless bed was not a new invention. But Catullus is not simply confessing that he has the hots for Calvus: the point of the poem is subtler than that. In using these clichés to describe his condition he is saying that the sweet session of amatory composition has backfired; the weapon the poet would turn on others has been turned back on him. Calvus' poetic cleverness has so excited him that he has been hoisted on his own petard, left in a state like—but not the same as—that of a thwarted lover, full of excitement but with no possibility of release. At last his poetic tension discharges itself in a poetic spasm:

> But when my limbs, exhausted by their labor,
> lay on the bed in nearly fatal stillness,
> I made this poem for you, my beloved,
> so you could take the measure of my sorrow.
> I beg you to be kind to my petition,
> darling, for if you aren't, if you're cruel,
> then Nemesis will turn on you in outrage.
> Don't rile her up, please—she's a bitch, that goddess.
>   [14–21]

The lover's language Catullus uses is part of the joke, but the acute reflectiveness of this poem should indicate that the favor he seeks is poetic rather than sexual, though of course it may have been that too. The poem begins with a self-conscious description of his feelings while he and his friend were composing verses. The clichés he uses to convey the effects are characteristic of the poetry they had been writing, which at the end becomes the very poem he writes to relieve those feelings. The proper response to his invitation is another poem that will reply in similar terms: the game must continue.

I suggested that this poem might have been seen as a neoteric manifesto for championing the values of playfulness and leisurely self-indulgence over the unacknowledged duties and obligations of public life. But I suspect that its vigorous projection of the erotic joys of poetic collaboration and its explicit defense of the dialogic nature of poetry might have been equally important to Catullus and the neoterics, and just as upsetting to people like Cicero.

Whether written in solitude or collaboration, the poem involves writer and reader in a spirit of mutual playfulness that is always at least implicitly erotic. In our earnest English, we "make" love and poetry, but when Catullus speaks of these activities together in poem 68, he uses the verb *ludere*, to play: *multa satis lusi*, "I had my fill of those games." It may seem unnecessary to belabor the playfulness of Catullus' verse: most readers will concede the point at once. Nevertheless, the critical implications of that playfulness have not yet been fully explored, and many critics still read his poems as though they were utterly straightforward, uncomplicated by irony and ambiguity. Catullus was an impressively complex blend of passion and cerebrality, and to understand the playfulness of his poems the reader must see both aspects of his nature at once. In the wake of Romanticism, however, it is easier to see and approve of the passionate Catullus, and most critics do. Poem 60, for instance, appears to be a fragment of pure feeling, a cry wrenched from the poet's heart:

Num te leaena montibus Libystinis
aut Scylla latrans infina inguinum parte

tam mente dura procreavit ac taetra,
ut supplicis vocem in novissimo casu
contemptam haberes, a nimis fero corde?

Either a lioness from Libya's mountains
or Scylla barking from her terrible bitch-womb
gave birth to you, so foul and so hard your heart is!
The great contempt you show as I lie here dying
with not a word from you! Such a bestial coldness.

[1–5]

Remarks E. T. Merrill, "Perhaps it was the last verse penned by Catullus as his strength failed him and death came on."[5] Perhaps. The armchair Romantic has no trouble imagining the fatal scene of the stylus slipping out of the cold hand on *corde*. But G. P. Goold, an editor and translator of Catullus, recently noted a clue that had been overlooked for at least the past seven hundred years: if you read down the first letters of each line and then read up the last letters, you find a telegraphically terse acrostic message: *natu ceu aes*, by birth like bronze—just as cold, just as unyielding.[6] Even on his deathbed then (if we take Catullus at his word here) an almost disembodied self-consciousness weaves its message into the emotional fabric of the poem.

The playfulness of Catullus' verse no doubt reflects the playfulness of his own sensibility, and of course it was an important part of the neoteric program, the legacy of their Roman antecedent Laevius and of the Alexandrians, who insisted that playfulness was preferable to pedagogy. "Every poet aims at charming, not instructing," as Eratosthenes said. That was a polemical statement, a shot fired across the bow of the Stoic insistence on poetry's educational function and value. But was it not also an admission that there is something about the way in which language is often used in poetry that makes it not entirely trustworthy as an instrument of instruction? The playfulness of poetry is in its language, and the play in poetic language admits what the earnest pedagogue denies: we don't always say what we mean or mean what we say.

There is nothing ironic or ambiguous about a punch in the nose from the point of view of the recipient of the action. The immediate effects of such a blow commonly include the disordering of the senses Catullus experiences at the sight of Lesbia in poem 51, closely followed by pain. We recognize a significant difference between an actual punch in the nose and a threat like "I'm gonna punch you in the nose!" Threats fall into the broad category of discourse whose subject is the relations between speakers, which Gregory Bateson calls "metacommunicative discourse" in his "Notes Toward a Theory of Fantasy and Play."[7]

By definition, a threat refers to something which does not yet exist: in the case above, the threat refers to a potential punch in the nose, and if we wished to determine the likelihood that the potential punch would become an actual one, we would have to draw on our knowledge of the relation between the two individuals involved. Moreover, we would have to interpret the wide range of nonverbal metacommunicative signals transmitted by stance, gesture, and body language that accompany the threat. And of course we would also have to consider that audience even now gathering for the possibility of momentary excitement; the presence of onlookers can exaggerate or provoke metacommunicative speech and gesture as each party attempts to enlist the audience on his side. The audience, not restricted to being spectators, can participate in the event by urging on or by inhibiting the violence.

It is usually easy to distinguish the threat from the punch. One step further removed from the threat is the poem that threatens to punch: like the threat, the poem refers to an as yet nonexistent punch; it is also a metacommunicative signal between two individuals and is often launched in the presence of an audience. But what distinguishes the threatening poem, found so commonly in the Book of Catullus, from the mere

threat? The answer, I believe, is that seemingly menacing poetry transmits another, more abstract set of metacommunicative signals, and those signals allow us to recognize such
poetry as a kind of play.

In Bateson's view, metacommunicative speech is possible
only because we are able to distinguish between mood-signs,
which are given involuntarily and are not subject to conscious
control or manipulation, and signals, which are voluntarily
given, consciously controlled, and manipulable. The aggres-
sive display of the male Siamese fighting fish at the sight of
another male (or at the sight of his own reflection in a mirror)
is a mood-sign; the headline in today's *New York Post* is a signal,
though its author would no doubt prefer his readers to respond
to it as a sign. Bateson first became aware of the crucial ability
to distinguish between mood-signs and signals while standing
in front of the monkey cage in San Francisco's Fleishhacker
Zoo; watching two young primates monkeying around, it suddenly struck him that such play "could only occur if the par-
ticipant organisms were capable of some degree of meta-
communication, i.e., of exchanging signals which would carry
the message 'this is play.'"

But in the statement "this is play," Bateson notes the elements of a paradox. "The playful nip denotes the bite, but it
does not denote what would be denoted by the bite." For
monkeys as for human beings, play is an activity in which consciously offered, explicit or implicit (that is, verbal and nonverbal) metacommunicative signals are exchanged between
individuals. These signals stand for other events, and as a result, as Bateson says, we notice that "the signals are untrue
because of the difference in denotation between the playful nip
and the real bite; they refer not to an actual bite, but to a future,
potential bite, or, more accurately, to the relationship between
the two individuals playing."

The statement "this is play" generates a paradoxical psy-
chological frame in which the actions of play have their context. Like all frames, it includes certain messages and, at the

same time, excludes others. It organizes our perceptions and tells us, in effect, "Attend to what is within and do not attend to what is outside." The frame also tells us that we are to attend to what is within *in a different way* than we would normally attend to what is outside: "The viewer . . . is not to use the same sort of thinking in interpreting the picture that he might use in interpreting the wallpaper outside the frame." The frame, then, is also a system of metacommunicative signals: the messages that define a frame also supply a context for understanding them; those messages also define the frame which includes them.

Almost any play situation illustrates Bateson's paradigm: for example, a father playing with his three-year-old son strikes an exaggerated posture of threat and says, "I'm gonna getcha!" The child squeals with delighted terror and runs off to hide. These games reveal two paradoxical components: a physical threat directed against the child and the framework of play in which those menacing gestures are set. The frame both defines and modifies the threat: the child understands that this is a play situation. The statement "this is play" occurs in the form of what Bateson calls implicit metacommunicative gestures, that is, the body language of the father, and in particular the use of exaggeration.

Bateson points out that the frame separating play from reality is often wobbly and in danger of breaking down. When two people stand on either side of a tennis net or sit down to a game of chess, they implicitly accept a frame that defines their subsequent actions as play. Most chess games and tennis matches remain securely within this framework: in other areas of our lives the frame is often more questionable and in danger of breaking down altogether, and much of our pleasure in play comes from our need for reassurance about the clarity of the signals exchanged. Bateson argues that this insecurity "leads us to the recognition of a more complex form of play: the game which is constructed not upon the premise 'This is play' but rather around the question 'Is this play?'"

Catullan playfulness is clearly interrogative rather than declarative, and so we often find ourselves asking, as we read him, "Does he really mean this?" At this point, let us return to the beginning of poem 16, about whose seriousness we wondered near the end of chapter III:

> Pedicabo ego vos et irrumabo,
> Aureli pathice et cinaede Furi

Once again, my paraphrase of these lines: "I will rape the both of you as each of you prefers it: you rectally, anal-receptive Furius, and you orally, oral-receptive Aurelius." Furius and Aurelius are being threatened with the most humiliating punishment one man could inflict on another in ancient Rome. The question "Does Catullus really mean it?" surfaces at once. We must attempt to answer it without knowing anything about the relation between these two and Catullus or whether the violence of his threat had been qualified by the circumstances of its occasion. Was the threat made in the course of a Saturnalian party where such verbal indecencies were perfectly acceptable? But this is neither the punch nor the threatened punch: it is a poem that threatens. As such, it transmits both the threat of violence and simultaneously a set of abstract metacommunicative signals that frame the threat and allow us to recognize it as the "more complex form of play" Bateson described as "constructed around the question, 'Is this play?'" These signals are further confined by the limits of poetic conventions. Whatever else it may be, a Catullan poem is primarily a grammatically ordered composition of words, arranged in lines of predetermined length according to an artificial prosodic system governing the distribution of long and short syllables in those lines. In this particular poem, the complexity of the surrounding rhetorical signals modifies the violence of the threat, which is delivered in two uncommonly elegant lines of verse, governed by chiastic inversion. The verbs at each end of the first line balance one another perfectly, framing the two pronouns within; we also notice a parallel arrangement in the way the two names in the second line are held in suspension, brack-

eting the two words describing Furius' and Aurelius' sexual
predilections:

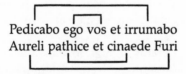

Pedicabo ego vos et irrumabo
Aureli pathice et cinaede Furi

However, since Aurelius prefers oral intercourse and Furius
prefers anal, the lines are further governed by an equally elegant diagonal chiasmus, one Alexander Pope would have ap-
preciated:

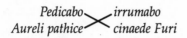

Pedicabo   *irrumabo*
Aureli pathice   *cinaede Furi*

One cannot read these lines as threat plus tropes: rather, the
obscene violence of the language and the rhetorical sophistication of its arrangement form a paradox that cannot be dis-
mantled. That paradox creates the tension sustaining the
poem's difficult balance between the possibilities of meaning—he really means it! he can't be serious!—alternatives the
poem must carefully balance.

In Catullus' poems it is often the most violent threats, the
most grotesquely distorted images of the body, and the most
obscene castigations that summon the most elegant strategies
as a counterbalance to keep the playful frame intact. We observe the same tension between message and metacommunicative signals, at an extreme, in poem 97, where Catullus
discusses a certain Aemilius:

> Really, I shouldn't have thought it made any difference
>   whether Aemilius opened his mouth or his asshole:
> one wouldn't expect to find elegance wafting from
>   either.
>   However, his asshole *does* show greater refinement,
> for it has no teeth. The teeth in his mouth are
>   enormous,
>   set maladroitly in gums of saddlebag leather,

and when (as he's wont to) he grins, one thinks of the
     gaping
  cunt of a she-mule in heat, pissing profusely.
He fucks a great many women and thinks himself
     charming,
  but hasn't brains enough to walk a miller's donkey.
Surely the woman who went with him ought to take
     pleasure
  in licking clean a sickly old hangman's asshole.

                                                    [1–12]

The paradox arises from the tension between the hair-raising obscenities of the poet's description of Aemilius and the measured
deliberation with which they are detailed, from the mild par-
enthetical oath of the first line to the horrifying scatology that
ends the poem. Catullus could be debating the merits of two
schools of oratory rather than destroying a person's reputation.

The issue of exaggeration arises in poem 97 where, as in
poem 16, the seriousness of the actual physical threat must be
justified by its provocation. What was the offense of Furius
and Aurelius? Catullus explains:

I'll fuck the pair of you as you prefer it,
oral Aurelius, anal Furius,
who read my verses but misread their author:
you think that *I'm* effeminate, since *they* are!
Purity's proper in the godly poet,
but it's unnecessary in his verses,
which really should be saucy and seductive,
even salacious in a girlish manner
and capable of generating passion
not just in boys, but in old men who've noticed
getting a hard-on has been getting harder!
But you, because my poems beg for kisses,
thousands of kisses, you think I'm a fairy!   [1–13]

Their offense is literary: they have misread several of Catullus'
poems, most likely poems 5 and 7, which, famously, deal with

kisses. Their accusation and his threat both involve sexual passivity. Because those poems are of a tender nature, Furius and
Aurelius have mistakenly assumed that their author is also
passively effeminate.

Much has been made of lines 5 and 6: in what sense can
Catullus describe himself as a *chaste* poet? Clearly, the word in
this context is ironic; a chaste poet would never make the
threat Catullus has just made. The inappropriate adjective
makes an even stronger case for distinguishing the effects his
verses have on others from the blameless mind that composed
them. We are moving the poem farther away from the punch
in the nose: the poet may say whatever he likes without being
held responsible for it. His words are privileged within the
playful framework of the poem. And just in case anyone has
missed the point, Catullus drives it home in his conclusion,
striking a note of mockery by repeating his opening lines: *pedicabo ego vos et irrumabo*.

Catullus indicates how the poem ought to be read when
he argues that, while it is proper for the poet to be chaste, his
verses should be seductive. If the poet's character does not appear in his verse, if his poems do not edify by presenting moral
truths, and if in fact their purpose is to arouse sluggish libidos,
then the poet would seem to have no responsibility for accurately depicting the world outside the poem.

We are getting close here to modernist notions of the self-
referential work of art, and while I don't want to overstate the
case, it seems clear that for Catullus the poet's responsibility
lies within the poem rather than outside it. What he tells us
about Furius and Aurelius may or may not be true: it doesn't
matter. The poet's concern is with making the poem more ef-
fective through vivid description. Exaggeration—or out-and-
out lying, for that matter—is not simply permissible but is to
be encouraged. We are not to judge the truth of the charges
brought against Furius and Aurelius or the accusation against
Aemilius: our approbation rests on the intensity with which
these charges are presented. And so, those who dismiss the
obscenity of the first two lines of poem 16 as nothing more than

Catullus' saying "Go to hell, the pair of you!" miss the point. The highly specific obscenities are as necessary to the effectiveness of the poem as is the chiastic arrangement. The obscenity contrasts with the rhetorical signals to establish the paradox of frame and context, the field of the poem as play, in which what is said is both meant and not meant, true and not true at the same time. What goes on outside that field concerns the moralist, not the poet.

But in order to complete our discussion of the poems of abuse, we must venture beyond the verses to their purposes and to the audience for whom they were intended. Ostensibly, their purpose would seem simple: to compel the person to whom the poem is addressed to alter his or her behavior. The abuse directed against Furius and Aurelius appears related to their purported interest in Catullus' young lover, Juventius. The poet attempts to mobilize the attention of an audience beyond the immediate recipients of the abuse. Although the poet addresses one or two people directly, he actually goes over their heads, as it were, to a wider audience whose understanding of the poem and approval of its message humiliate the recipient.

We see the paradigm illustrated in poem 42, addressed to an unnamed woman who seems to have stolen the writing tablets on which Catullus composed his verses:

> Up now, iambics—get yourselves together,
> all of you everywhere, however many!
> —A flaming slut imagines that she'll mock me,
> and now refuses to return the tablets
> I write you verses down on—can you bear it?
> Let's follow her and force her to return them.
> Who're you after? *her*—that one you see there,
> shaking her ass and mouthing like a mimic,
> the rabid bitch with the repulsive grimace!
> Surround her now and force her to return them:
> *You wretched slut you give us back the tablets,*
> *give us the tablets back you wretched slut you!*

Doesn't that bother you? you filth, you flophouse,
you drain on even *my* profound invective!
—We mustn't think we've gotten satisfaction:
if nothing else, at least we can embarrass
the bitch and give her cheeks a little color.
Cry out once more, in unison and louder:
You wretched slut you give us back the tablets,
give us the tablets back you wretched slut you!
We're getting nowhere. Nothing seems to move her.
Maybe we ought to try another tactic
and see if it won't work a little better:
Maiden most modest, give us back the tablets.   [1–24]

At the heart of this poem is a paradox: imagine a woman so
depraved that the only insult she responds to is the accusation
of virtue. But while the poem addresses the woman, Catullus
goes over her head to the hendecasyllabic verses that are at
once the instrument of her torment and the audience for her
humiliation—a thronging crowd that surrounds her and repeats the poet's accusations.

In a variation on this approach, Catullus ignores the target
of the poem completely in poem 97. The unspeakable Aemilius
is not addressed directly for the good reason that a man too
stupid to guide a miller's donkey would hardly be able to
understand as elaborate a verbal artifact as this poem. By ignoring him, by speaking over his head, the poet finds yet another way to add to his humiliation. The truth of the matter is
unimportant: "Nothing more is known of this Aemilius,"
writes E. T. Merrill.[8]

What more would anyone want to know of him?

Bateson's description of the "two peculiarities of play" is
worth keeping in mind here: "The message or signals exchanged in play are in a certain sense untrue or not meant; and
. . . that which is denoted by these signals is nonexistent."
Reading the short poems of Catullus, the last point is hard to
ignore: Catullus is the least retrospective of poets and one

could virtually define his short poems by saying that they are about something which has not yet happened.

But the reader must also keep in mind the double-edged nature of playful statements: they mean what they say, and at the same time they do not mean what they say. This ambiguity of meaning limits the commitments possible in this kind of poetry, for the fact is that we do not only ask, "does he really mean it?" when we come across an outrageous obscenity, as in poems 16 or 56; if we have any sense at all, we ask the question at the beginning of poem 3 where Catullus summons Venuses, Cupids, and all mortals who share their refinement to mourn the death of his lady's sparrow. We also query the poet's sincerity at the beginning of poem 5 when Catullus invites Lesbia to live solely for loving. Why shouldn't we ask it?—Lesbia certainly did. For in love as in war, there is a distinction between the actual kiss and the proposition floated by the ardent swain, and a further distinction between these two cases and the poem in which Catullus begs his beloved for thousands and hundreds of kisses, as in poem 5:

> Give me a thousand kisses, then a hundred,
> another thousand next, another hundred,
> a thousand without pause and then a hundred   [7–9]

Does he really mean it? Lesbia herself asked, apparently, because Catullus begins the next poem in the sequence of which this is a part with her rejoinder:

> My Lesbia, you ask how many kisses
> would be enough to satisfy or sate me?   [7, 1–2]

Her question might have been more on the order of, "Really, Catullus! What *do* you have in mind?"

Nevertheless, in the erotic poems as in the poems of abuse, we find that exaggeration in the service of persuasion is no vice. Distortions of scale, number, and frequency abound, whether Catullus is referring to the innumerable kisses he will have from Lesbia before he is satisfied or to the two hundred lovers of poem 11 who cannot satisfy the now insatiable Lesbia.

But beyond such exaggerations and distortions, a number of the polymetric poems function rather mysteriously, as mirrors, their meanings entirely dependent on what their readers make of them. We can account for them only by assuming that Catullus understood the usefulness of this kind of poem and deliberately exploited the possibilities of multiple meanings. Earlier I discussed the ambiguities in poems 41 and 43, as well as G. P. Goold's discovery of the acrostic in poem 60. But poem 49, addressed to Cicero, compares in ingenuity:

> Most eloquent of all the past and present
> offspring of Romulus, o Marcus Tullu,
> —and of all those to come in future ages!
> you've won the gratitude of your Catullus,
> who is most certainly the worst of poets;
> as certainly the very worst of poets
> as you are—certainly—the best of lawyers. [1–7]

Is this an uncomplicated expression of heartfelt gratitude, or a clever put-down of Cicero, a poem disguised as abject flattery with a trap set and baited in the last two lines? The poem is so perfectly balanced between the two possibilities that it cannot answer my question by tilting in one direction or the other. Catullus certainly intended to write a poem Cicero would find problematic, a poem whose meaning would depend on Cicero's reading of it. And Cicero would have read it: the poem that is now between two pages was once, in Frank O'Hara's telling phrase, between two persons. How would Cicero have responded? The most appealing scenario would have canny Cicero receive the poem, not knowing whether he is being tweaked for his susceptibility to flattery or flattered sincerely. Accordingly, he avoids Catullus for a day or two while he figures out an equally ambivalent response, but when he next meets Catullus and broaches the subject of the poem, Catullus pretends not to know what Cicero is talking about.

There are to be sure other scenarios, but playfulness is

always an invitation to a dialogue, and the meaning of a poem that embraces playfulness has less to do with the words on the page than with the relations between writer and reader.

In discussing playfulness, I have for the most part discussed the polymetric poems as the best examples of it in Catullus' poetry. Many of the elegiac epigrams, on the other hand, seem to have been written as antidotes to that playfulness. They are satirical or analytical instruments of discovery and correction, sent out into the social world to set right a serious disjunction between reality as perceived by Catullus and reality as misunderstood by someone else.

Although as various in their subjects and in their recipients as the polymetric poems are, the elegiac epigrams are composed on a few basic premises. One of these is a mysterious situation, puzzling to Catullus or another person, suddenly clarified. Thus, in poem 69, Rufus has been wondering why he is so unsuccessful with the ladies; Catullus reveals the source of Rufus' problem in his goatlike body odor. In poem 80, people have been speculating about a certain peculiarity of Gellius' appearance; Catullus reveals its source in Gellius' perverse sexual appetite. Rufus and Gellius both behave in ways they don't understand, oblivious of the effects on others. The discovery and correction of similar lapses in self-awareness is the burden of many elegiac epigrams.

Almost any handful of the elegiac epigrams will show the considerable range of situations in which the poet uses the poetic form to close the gap between delusion and reality. In poem 81, Catullus' young lover Juventius has thrown the poet over for someone less suitable, unaware of the consequences for Catullus:

> Was there no one, Juventius? No one? In all of the city,
>   no darling man for you to go fall in love with,
> besides this houseguest of yours from decaying
>   Pisaurum,
>   this stranger more jaundiced than a gilded statue?

Now you adore him and dare to thrust him before us,
ignorant of what a criminal thing you are doing!
[1–6]

In poem 82, a certain Quintius is trying to steal a lover from
Catullus, ignorant of that person's importance to Catullus:

Quintius, if you wish Catullus to owe you his eyes or
anything dearer to him than even his eyes are,
keep your hands off what is dearer to him than his eyes
or
dearer than anything dearer than his eyes are. [1–4]

In poem 83, as we have seen, Lesbia's mate does not perceive
the true meaning of his wife's verbal abuse of the poet:

Lesbia hurls abuse at me in front of her husband:
that fatuous person finds it highly amusing!
Nothing gets through to you, jackass—for silence would
signal
that she'd been cured of me, but her barking and
bitching
shows that not only haven't I not been forgotten,
but that this burns her: and so she rants and rages.
[1–6]

And in poem 84, hapless Arrius, everyone's favorite nouveau,
is unaware of the effect that his ostentatious huffing has on
those who know better:

Arrius had to have aitches to swell his orations,
and threatened us all with 'hawful hinsidias
hachshuns!'
He flattered himself on account of his great aspirations,
for huffing as hard as he could, 'Hit's hinsidious!'
He got it, I guess, from his mother or his freeborn uncle
or else from others of his mother's poor relations.
Our ears were relieved to learn he'd been sent off to
Syria:

> they still heard the same words, but without the hard
>   breathing.
> No longer fearful of hearing such speech in the future,
>   we got, quite suddenly, a horrible message:
> after the journey of Arrius, the huffed-at Ionian
>   sea had acquired an aitch: now it's Hionian!   [1–10]

These epigrams are all directed at others, but in Catullus'
hands the poems became powerful instruments for examining
the complexities of his own experience, thought, and emotions, perhaps most famously in poem 85:

> I hate and love. And if you should ask how I can do both,
>   I couldn't say; but I feel it, and it tortures me.   [1–2]

The urgency of his quest for self-understanding and the acute-
ness of his discoveries are both evident in poem 72:

> You used to say that you wished to know only Catullus,
>   Lesbia, and wouldn't take even Jove before me!
> I didn't regard you just as my mistress then: I cherished
>   you
>   as a father does his sons or his daughters' husbands.
> Now that I know you, I burn for you even more fiercely,
>   though I regard you as almost utterly worthless.
> How can that be, you ask? it's because such cruelty
>   forces
>   lust to assume the shrunken place of affection. [1–8]

Like poem 83, poem 72 fits into a distinct subset of the
epigrams whose premise might be paraphrased as "Lesbia
says (or said) one thing, but she really means (or meant) something very different." Poem 70 gives us another version of the
charge raised against Lesbia in poem 72:

> My woman says there is no one whom she'd rather
>   marry
>   than me, not even Jupiter, if he came courting.

> That's what she says—but what a woman says to a
>   passionate lover
> ought to be scribbled on wind, on running water.
>   [1–4]

Words that say what the speaker really means can be engraved
on tablets or at least written down on papyrus, but Lesbia's
declaration of intent is language at play, words that at the same
time mean and do not mean what they say. The poet can express this paradox only through another paradox: her words
should be written on those elements that will not sustain them.
In poem 72, Catullus describes his feeling for her in ways that
differ from the unsponsored, unsanctified feelings of a man
for a mistress: "I cherished you / as a father does his sons or
his daughters' husbands." The point is not simply that these
are not sexual relationships, but that they are relationships
guaranteed by blood and by the most solemn vows to heaven.
    Such oaths become the poet's model for a kind of speech
that is emptied of the deception of playfulness, speech in
which there is the same kind of relation between utterance and
intended effect as there is in prayer. He makes this clear in
poem 76:

> If any pleasure can come to a man through recalling
>   decent behavior in his relations with others,
> not breaking his word, and never, in any agreement,
>   deceiving men by abusing vows sworn to heaven,
> then countless joys will await you in old age, Catullus,
>   as a reward for this unrequited passion!   [1–6]

Proper behavior consists in keeping one's word, whether offered to gods or men, and even though the third couplet is
probably ironic, it draws on the notion of a piety whose essential feature is that truthful words and deeds are rewarded.
After complaining that Lesbia's vileness has made his words
and deeds worthless, Catullus exhorts himself to break off
with her completely and concludes with a prayer. Here is the
end of play, of playfulness, of playing around: the gods will

not be mocked. Here is language as it ought to be used, and in exchange for piety, a prayer to be answered:

> O gods, if pity is yours, or if ever to any
>   who lay near death you offered the gift of your mercy
> look on my suffering: if my life seems to you decent,
>   then tear from within me this devouring cancer,
> this heavy dullness wasting the joints of my body,
>   completely driving every joy from my spirit!
> Now I no longer ask that she love me as I love her,
>   or—even less likely—that she give up the others:
> all that I ask for is health, an end to this foul sickness!
>   O gods, grant me this in exchange for my devotion.
>   [17–26]

For Catullus the act of poetry was a process, a continual interaction between the poet and the members of his audience. We would scarcely expect serious poetry to be inspired by social obligation, but nothing would have been more natural for him.

Poem 65 was composed for a man named Ortalus, who had apparently written Catullus to ask for some new poems. In response, Catullus informs Ortalus that because of the recent death of his brother he is unable to write anything. The fact that he replies in a self-consciously composed verse-epistle should not mislead us into supposing that this is either trivial or artificial; it is neither. The poem begins with the poet in the depths of his sorrow:

> Though I'm exhausted by grief, by the unbroken sorrow
>   that calls me away from the poetic virgins,
> and too overwhelmed with my troubles to fetch you out
>   any
>   sweet signs of new life from the Muses, Ortalus—
> for only a short while ago the pale foot of my brother
>   sank in the flowing waters of pitiless Lethe:

snatched from my sight, he lies restless under the alien
soil of the Troad, below the beach at Rhoeteum.

[1–8]

In poem 50 the act of poetic composition was described as a
sexual embrace; here, poems become the product of that embrace. The intensity of the poet's grief has estranged him from
the Muses and he is unable to display any of their sweet offspring to Ortalus. At this point, Catullus' brother is quite recently dead. These lines emphasize the suddenness of that
death: his brother has been "snatched from my sight"; he lies
concealed under the earth and can only be glimpsed in a met-
onymic figure, his "wretched, pale foot" seen as he steps into
the waters of Lethe to wade to Charon's waiting ferry. Lethe,
which washed away the memories of his brother's past life,
was the border of the underworld, which of course gives us
another indication of the recentness of his brother's death.

But Catullus cannot remain in this place forever even in
his imagination, and must retrace his path to the world of the
living. The poem that began in bereavement goes on to record
the necessary process of healing. The first step is to come to
terms with his sudden loss and then to find an appropriate
way to make his brother's death a part of his own life:

. . . .
never again will I set eyes on you, brother
more dear than life is: but surely I will always love you
always your death will have its place in my singing
as the nightingale sings under the dense-shadowed
branches,
mourning the fate of Itylus, gone from beside her.

[10–14]

Although their physical separation is final, his brother's death
can be transformed through the poet's art, thus adding the
poignancy of mourning to his song. In the legend to which
Catullus alludes, Procne, the wife of Tereus, avenges her husband's violation of her sister, Philomela, by slaying their son,

Itylus. When Tereus pursues the sisters, the gods change
Procne into a nightingale and Philomela into a swallow. It is
for this reason that the beauty of the nightingale's singing is
the beauty of lamentation, the burden of sorrow transformed
into the clarity of song.

Once that burden has been accepted and transformed,
Catullus can return to the world of his social obligations, the
most pressing of which is his duty to write poetry for his
friends:

> Nevertheless, in my sorrow, Ortalus, I send you
>   a poem which I've translated from Callimachus,
> so that you shouldn't imagine your words had been
>   scattered
>   to the aimless winds, put from my mind and
>   forgotten.   [15–18]

We see here the poet beginning to recover from his grief; unable to write something of his own, he will send a translation
from his favorite, Callimachus, for Ortalus must not think that
his request had been forgotten.

> just as the apple, a gift on the sly from her lover,
>   falls from the perfectly blameless lap of the virgin:
> oblivious wretch! she'd hidden it under her gown, but
>   rises politely, seeing her mama—and sends it
> hurtling out of its hiding place, bouncing and rolling
>   while a self-conscious scarlet flows over her sad face!
>   [19–24]

This unusually elaborate simile is not merely decoration
to close a verse epistle, but rather a figure that represents the
resolution of the process of mourning that the poet has traced
through the poem. Having passed through the bleak stage of
initial bereavement and having seen that he must incorporate
his grief over the loss of his brother into his art, Catullus is
now summoned by his obligation to Ortalus to perform his
social function as a poet. That obligation is nothing less than
a summons back to life. In his bereavement, Catullus has been

unable to display the offspring of the muses, the *dulcis fetus Musarum*. The word *fetus* refers to the bringing forth of young, but also to fruits and vegetables, and to the sweet fruits of those learned virgins, the Muses. Catullus is their thwarted suitor, unable in his grief to court them, to tempt them to bring forth those fruits that lie repressed. Their concealment corresponds to his brother's body under the earth and to the eradication of the brother's memory by the waters of Lethe.

As Catullus is summoned back to life and as he consents to that summons by providing Ortalus with the one gift that he is capable of offering, another gift comes forth spontaneously, unbidden, in the last six lines of the poem. Metaphor is a poetic way of knowing: "If I were to forget my obligation to Ortalus, I would be like—what? Why, like that virgin." The relation between the poet and his Muses at the beginning of the poem is balanced by the relation between the lover and the virgin of the closing simile: both involve the withholding of gifts. Repression of memory leads back to death, to the waters of Lethe. But the summons is to life: as the girl is called to life by her lover, Catullus is summoned by Ortalus. Both must be answered. The girl conceals the apple in her lap, showing the sexual nature of her irresolution. That which is repressed—in Catullus, the gift of poetry—must be revealed: the girl rises at the sight of her mother and the apple tumbles out from under her tunic, as though she had given birth to it. The apple tumbles forward in a bewildering rush, its action mimicked, in the Latin of the original, by a bewildering rush of spondaic verses, themselves the sweet offspring of the Muses.

V INVITATIONS AND EXCORIATIONS

One of the most persistently recurring tendencies in the body of critical comment that has shaped our understanding of Catullus in modern times has been that of seeing his sensibility as fundamentally divided: A. L. Wheeler spoke of "an intellectual Catullus side by side with an emotional Catullus . . . who gave himself recklessly to the enjoyment of life."[1] Wilhelm Kroll noted the same split in the poet's sensibility but cast the opposing figures in more dramatic fashion, turning the intellectual Catullus into an "Alexandrian weighed down by the burden of tradition" and the emotional Catullus into a "spontaneous, primitive child of nature."[2]

Living after not only the age of Eliot but the Pound era as well, we might be inclined to see the Alexandrian Catullus, the poet as shaper and transmitter of his cultural heritage, as the more valuable or at least the more interesting of the two; however, this was certainly not the prevailing opinion among earlier scholars and editors who discounted or dismissed the poet's cerebrality, the better to see him as spontaneous songbird, creature of instinct and passion. Their Catullus, as E. T. Merrill put it, did not study life but felt it, "swayed by its ever-changing emotions," and his childlike nature was "warm in quick affections, hot in swift hatreds, pulsing with the most active red blood."[3] That other Catullus—the one with the brain—could now be safely pensioned off: whatever functions he may at one time have performed would be taken over by those who study him, a point made by William Butler Yeats in his poem about Catullus called, appropriately, "The Scholars":

Bald heads forgetful of their sins,
Old, learned, respectable bald heads
Edit and annotate the lines
That young men, tossing on their beds,
Rhymed out in love's despair
To flatter beauty's ignorant ear. . . .

Lord, what would they say
Did their Catullus walk that way?[4]

The "two-Catullus" theory persists due to the tendency of some classicists to see the literary manifestations of Alexandrian influence as the dead hand of academic obscurantism stifling the poetic impulse. But this dual view of the poet also results from the fact that throughout the nineteenth century poetry increasingly came to be identified with lyric verse, and the popular anthologies of the day especially prized lyric verse in which sentiment and the simplicity of song took precedence over thought and the complexities of speech. This attitude shaped the taste of the reading public well into our own century, *pace* modernism and the modernists. In such a critical climate, one did not advance the cause of one's poet by arguing—or even by admitting—that he was capable of self-consciousness.

The reaction against the two-Catullus theory was led by Kenneth Quinn in his influential book *The Catullan Revolution*, which appeared in 1959. Quinn provided Catullan criticism with a notion of the intellectual complexity possible in poetry that could be described, despite that complexity, as lyric. Quinn also insisted on seeing the poet's work whole, the product of an undivided sensibility. Refusing to "chop the poetry of Catullus into two chunks," he proposed an analysis based on "what may be called differing *levels of intent*, differing degrees of devotion to the task of making poetry, varying, in the case of Catullus, from the most casual versifying to the most complete surrender to inspiration."[5]

Quinn's formulation addresses the response that modern readers of Catullus typically have to his short poems; some of them appear to be bizarre or trivial, while others are important lyric statements. Quinn's notion of "levels of intent" brings with it, however, a new set of difficulties, for identifying these levels inevitably divides Catullus again in two, the trivial versifier as opposed to the wholly inspired poet. Other complications arise: How can we trace our way back from the poem to the inspiration which produced it? And why should we? How can we be sure that what appears to us as the most casual versifying did not in fact spring from the most complete surrender to inspiration, and vice versa? And finally, how can we be certain that surrender to inspiration will in every case yield a better poem than casual versifying?

Quinn's approach assumes that we can always understand the intentions of the poet and that the poems of Catullus are straightforward creatures that always say what they mean and mean what they say. Quinn ignores not only the possibilities of ambiguity but the presence of ironies large and small, and, most important, it ignores Catullan playfulness. What then are we to make of the "levels of intent"? If they are ultimately unsatisfactory critical tools, the impulse that lies behind them, the desire to see Catullus whole, is a valuable one. Not to do so results in well-meaning criticism that discusses Catullus as though his sensibility could be divided up and parceled out among neatly labeled entities—"the Lesbia poems," "the poems to Juventius," and so on—as though Catullus were goods in a department store rather than a poet. But if we are to see Catullus undivided, we must ask whether there is in the poems themselves a strategy that manifests the wholeness we seek.

The poems of Catullus are both willful and playful, continually thrusting their own intentions at us and thwarting our expectations of how poems ought to behave. Before analyzing that willfulness it might be useful to examine a different kind of poem, one that wholeheartedly embraces the expectations of its audience. That poem is the fifth ode of Horace, Book I:

> Quis multa gracilis te puer in rosa
> perfusus liquidis urget odoribus

> grato, Pyrrha, sub antro?
>   Cui flavam religas comam,
>
> simplex munditiis? Heu quotiens fidem
> mutatosque deos flebit et aspera
>   nigris aequora ventis
>   emirabitur insolens
>
> qui nunc te fruitur credulus aurea
> qui semper vacuam, semper amabilem
>   sperat, nescius aurae
>   fallacis. Miseri, quibus
>
> intemptata nites. Me tabula sacer
> votiva paries indicat uvida
>   suspendisse potenti
>   vestimenta maris deo.
>
> What energetic, artlessly aromatic
> adolescent urges you, presses you, Pyrrha,
>   in a surround of roses;
>   admires the blonde hair bound back,
>
> elegantly simple. Poor him. How very often
> will he lament the ancient verities vanquished
>   and gape in astonishment
>   as black winds roughen the smooth seas—
>
> Let's call him Credulus. He believes you're golden,
> ignores the deceptive glitter and imagines
>   you'll be his unconniving
>   darling, always. Wretched, those you
>
> dazzle, unventured. And me? The votive tablet
> on the temple wall shows that I've left the sodden
>   rags of former habit as
>   tribute to the sea god's power.[6]

We would not be likely to take this—or mistake it—for a modern poem. It presents itself as a model of poetic decorum, a triumphant instance of experience distilled into an achieved form, rather than a risk-taking venture in uttering the unut-

terable. Within these orderly metrical precincts Horace reca-
pitulates the terms of an erotic adventure, real or imagined,
through stages of passionate involvement (discreetly alluded
to rather than vulgarly displayed), disenchanting betrayal, and
ironic resignation.

Innumerable small graces attend the poet, and generations of teachers have exhausted themselves and their students
in admiring the exquisite (and inimitable, in English) arrangement of words in the poem's first line. The young woman (addressed as *te*) is embraced by the two words describing the new
love in her life (*gracilis te puer*). The loving couple is quite literally surrounded by that abundance of roses:

quis *multa* gracilis te puer *in rosa*

Nor can enough be said of the poet's skillful development of
the poem's central metaphor, the transformation of Pyrrha
from a simple flirt into a man-destroying force of nature. There
is even enough room in the poem to shelter an ambiguity: is
Horace complaining about Pyrrha's infidelity to him or about
the way she—and women like her—steal all the attractive
boys?

Such questions are unanswerable: the poem is governed
by a decorum that both suggests and conceals the pain Pyrrha
has caused Horace. On the other hand, that decorum may be
just a sign of the poet's sympathetic understanding of the relative lack of importance his culture attributes to such moments
in the erotic life.

The experience that provoked the poem is unimportant in
itself; what matters is the way it can be transformed into poetry. First, it must be purged of all traces of the contingent, the
conditional, the merely fortuitous: not for Horace the pleasure
that a poet like Wallace Stevens takes in the truly dizzying possibility that "Mrs. Anderson's Swedish baby / Might well have
been German or Spanish."[7] Horace's task is to polish the gritty
particularities of quotidian experience into reflective generali-
ties, for "the aim of the poet is to inform or delight or to com-

bine together in what he says, both pleasure and applicability to life."[8] We can enjoy singular instances, but we cannot learn from them as such: the sight of a man slipping on a banana peel may be amusing, but it does not teach us not to, or how not to, slip on banana peels. We learn only by generalizing from our repeated experiences.

And so Horace makes no attempt to confer individuality on his characters: *puer* and Pyrrha are purely generic: he's the Boy and she's the Blonde (her name in Greek means "the auburn-haired"). They are not real people but stereotypes caught up in an endlessly recurring pattern; if they were not thus enmeshed, we could not learn from them.

The poem continues to move farther away from the particular with the metaphor that transforms Pyrrha into a sea to which trusting mariners commit themselves only to perish when the weather changes without warning. That transformation (as well as the knowing certainty with which Horace describes her seductive activities at the beginning of the poem) suggests a process as cyclical as the changing seasons of the year. There will always be Pyrrha, or what Pyrrha represents, and there will also be *puer*, deceived by her elegant simplicity. From our understanding of the pattern they form when they coincide, we can both learn and take pleasure.

The transformation of experience into art requires the action of the poem to move from a somewhat distanced present of stereotypical characters in recurrent situations into a mythically valorized past. And so the poem concludes with the votive tablet displaying the consecrated signs of the poet's resignation, offered up as the rescued victims of shipwreck would offer their dripping garments to Neptune. That conclusion apotheosizes the experience, removes it from the plane of the contemporary and fixes it forever in the realm of the divine. But the image of the votive tablet also comes to stand for the poem that produced the image, a poem that has now completed its transformation of an experience of erotic unsuccess into an emblematic souvenir of the life of feeling, a souvenir not unlike the culturally weightier poetic memorial that Horace raised to the endurance of his own work: "I have completed a monument more lasting than bronze, loftier than the regal pyramids."[9]

The poem-as-souvenir memorializes an experience, projecting it backward into a mythical past where it will remain forever unchanged. Its analogies are permanent things, the marble and bronze of memorials or the stone of the votive tablet, in contrast to the contingent, accidental nature of a sudden storm and a thorough soaking. But when that experience is projected into the mythical past, the audience for this poem becomes, by a simultaneous act of forward projection, posterity. The poem-as-souvenir has no contemporary audience, no throng of gleeful or outraged bystanders responding to it as act or gesture. Those who hear it or read it—even those who once upon a time heard Horace himself read it—have been transformed into descendants whose task is to confer greatness upon the poet.

For Catullus, however, poetry is rarely a matter of experience recollected and transformed, in tranquillity or otherwise. If we were to choose a typical poem, it would probably be an invitation rather than a souvenir, such as poem 5:

> Lesbia, let us live only for loving,
> and let us value at a single penny
> all the loose flap of senile busybodies!   [1–3]

or the invitation extended to Fabullus in poem 13:

> You will dine well with me, my dear Fabullus,
> in a few days or so, the gods permitting   [1–2]

In poem 37 another friend, the poet Caecilius, is invited to visit Catullus in Verona:

> Go, poem, pay a call on Caecilius,
> my friend the master of erotic verses:
> tell him to leave his lakefront place at Comum
> and spend a little time here at Verona   [1–4]

And the invitation that seeks one in return from Ipsitilla in poem 32:

> I beg of you, my sweet, my Ipsitilla,
> my darling, my sophisticated beauty,
> invite me over for an assignation.   [1–3]

I am not exploiting a merely accidental resemblance here: these poems deliberately present themselves as invitations at the same time and to the same extent that they present themselves as poems. Other invitations are as different from these as these are from each other: in poem 3 we are invited to mourn the death of his mistress's sparrow, and in poem 31 Catullus invites beautiful lake Garda (on whose sapphire waters he is sailing) to join him in celebrating his homecoming. Flavius is invited to speak up in poem 6, likewise Camerius in poem 55. There are also a great many negative invitations in which Catullus invites someone to cease behavior he does not approve of; Asinius is "invited" to return the napkin he has stolen from the poet in poem 12, and Caesar is invited to share Catullus' indignation at the rapacity of Mamurra in poem 29. Often these negative invitations are coupled to withering excoriations of the sort directed against the firm of Vibennius & Son in poem 33:

> why don't you both go straight to hell together,
> now that the father's thefts are common knowledge,
> and you, son, have no hope of finding buyers
> who'll pay a penny for such hairy buttocks.   [5–8]

Given the intensely social nature of Catullus' poetry, the frequency of the poem-as-invitation, especially among the polymetric poems, is hardly a mystery. Cicero describes the smart set as made up of young men who never declined invitations to dinner, and in poem 47 Catullus comments briefly and ironically on the social importance of such invitations. Other poems deal with the perils of accepting such invitations without due regard for the literary propensities of one's host.

But these are poems *about* invitations, and our concern is

with those poems that *are* invitations. As such, they resemble the invitations that we commonly receive from and extend to our circle of lovers, friends, and acquaintances: these poems result from a desire to begin or continue a relationship with another person, though it is not necessary in the invitation to allude to either the desire or the relationship. Similarly, the poems-as-invitations anticipate and announce a particular occasion; they are meant for a specific person or persons and ordinarily cannot be transferred because their purpose is to persuade. Finally, they request, implicitly or explicitly, the favor of a response. The Catullan poems-as-invitations share these characteristics, which reveal their poet's articulation with his experience, his art, his audience. As invitations, the poems are inseparable from the evanescence of speech and gesture, inseparable as well from those to whom they are addressed and from the occasions they anticipate and proclaim.

The poem-as-invitation begins in, and emerges from, a dialogue between Catullus and another person to whom the poem is usually addressed. The dialogue consists of all the conversations that have taken place between the two, conversations that provide the context of their relationship. It also includes any conversation that they may have been engaged in at the moment before the poem, for the abrupt beginnings of many of the poems suggest an opportunistic leap into a pause in the exchange, a leap made when the relationship between the poet and the addressee is momentarily brought into sharp focus and the conversation intensifies into verse.

And so the poem-as-invitation consists of two parts: the spoken (or—more commonly—the unspoken) dialogue from which it emerges, and the invitation or excoriation, the burden that the poem must deliver. The dialogue is in effect the past tense of the relationship between Catullus and the recipient of the poem, while the invitation represents the present and future tenses of that relationship, a continuation of the dialogue by different means rather than a break with it.

In the poems, the proportion of dialogue to invitation is

highly variable; at times, the dialogue may be quite extensive, but more often than not it is suppressed altogether or only briefly alluded to, as in the poems I cited earlier. The presence or absence of dialogue seems to depend entirely on how much of the past relationship needs to be developed in the poem in order to account for the poet's present feelings and for the invitation itself.

Poem 32, for example, completely suppresses the dialogue:

> I beg of you, my sweet, my Ipsitilla,
> my darling, my sophisticated beauty,
> invite me over for an assignation;
> and, if you're willing, do me one big favor:
> don't let another client shoot the door bolt,
> and don't decide to suddenly go cruising,
> but stay at home and get yourself all ready
> for nine—yes, nine—successive copulations!
> Honestly, if you want it, give the order:
> I've eaten, and I'm sated, supinated!
> My prick is poking through my cloak and tunic. [1–11]

Obviously Catullus and Ipsitilla were previously acquainted; otherwise neither poem nor invitation would make sense. But that past dialogue is neither included nor alluded to in the poem, probably because Catullus thought it unnecessary; Ipsitilla's predilections were no doubt sufficiently known to the poet's immediate audience and an explanatory dialogue would have been redundant. This is often the case. Poem 22, which is not itself a poem-as-invitation, but a commentary on what happens when one accepts the invitation of the occasionally sufferable Suffenus, begins by acknowledging such a familiarity: *Suffenus iste, Vare, quem probe nosti*, "Varus, you know Suffenus as well as any."

From time to time, however, Catullus refers directly to the dialogue that precedes the poem, as in poem 7, which begins with Catullus' paraphrase of Lesbia's question:

> My Lesbia, you ask how many kisses
> Would be enough to satisfy, to sate me!   [1–2]

Here we could easily reconstruct the question to which the poem is both an answer and a further, implicit, probe. Poem 72, though not an invitation, also begins with the memory of an earlier dialogue between the lovers:

> You used to say that you wished to know only Catullus,
>   Lesbia, and wouldn't take even Jove before me!
>
>   [1–2]

An interesting variation on this pattern occurs in poem 35, which begins with Catullus' instructions to his sheet of papyrus. The page itself—and the very words we are reading—should invite his friend Caecilius to Verona for a visit:

> Go, page, and pay a call on Caecilius,
> my friend the master of erotic verses:
> tell him to leave his lakefront place at Comum
> and spend a little time here at Verona   [1–4]

Catullus is intriguingly inexplicit (or perhaps explicitly intriguing) about why he wishes to see his friend:

> for I have certain weighty cogitations
> to deliver—words from a friend of ours!   [5–6]

The remainder of the poem develops the invitation while allowing us to learn that Caecilius has a cultivated mistress and that he has an impressively good poem in progress, both of which Catullus finds worthy of his friend:

> —Wherefore, if he is wise, he'll get the lead out,
> although a thousand times his peerless lady
> should seize him, fling her arms about his neck, and
> beg him to linger in her soft embraces.
> That girl is crazy for him; if the story
> I've heard is true, she perishes of passion:
> for ever since she first read his unfinished
> poem, his epic Mistress of Dindymus,

> flames have been feeding on her deepest marrow.
> Lady more artful than the Sapphic Muse is,
> I feel for you! It really is exquisite,
> his almost finished poem on Cybele.   [7–18]

We do not learn why Catullus wants to see Caecilius so badly,
a lack of information that one critic tried to remedy by arguing
that Catullus is summoning Caecilius to tell him he should
stop spending so much time with the mistress and get on with
finishing the poem. One would tend to doubt that such advice
would ever have entered Catullus' mind; if it had, he could
have simply put it in the letter to Caecilius rather than drag his
friend all the way to Verona. But surely the poem as it stands
is persuasive in its lack of explicitness and yet explicit enough
for its occasion, the invitation to renew a dialogue on love and
poetry. The references to Caecilius' mistress and his poem on
Cybele show the intimacy of their past relationship, of secrets
shared and certain things left unsaid.

Although Catullus usually suppresses the dialogue lead-
ing up to the poem or alludes to it indirectly, poem 10 consists
almost entirely of dialogue. It offers an unusual illustration of
the relation between context and foreground, dialogue, and—
in this particular case—excoriation. Catullus has been idling
in the forum when he is led off by his old friend Varus to have
a look at Varus' new mistress:

> Ran into Varus over at the forum,
> just killing time. We went to see his girlfriend,
> who struck me right away as—well, a hooker,
> but fairly clever and not unattractive.   [1–4]

Almost immediately the subject of Bithynia comes up: clearly
Catullus has just returned from his journey, and Varus' girlfriend assumes that he has, as is usual in these cases, profited
from his experience. At first Catullus tries to tell her the truth,
which leads him into a lightheartedly obscene denunciation of
his patron, Memmius:

> I told them what the score was: natives nothing,
> nothing for governors or their lieutenants:
> no one comes back from there rolling in money—
> and that cornholing bastard we went out with
> just didn't give a damn about our pockets.   [9–13]

But Varus' girlfriend is unwilling to settle for the unadorned
truth; surely, she insists, surely Catullus must have returned
with some slaves to bear his litter. Catullus falls into the trap:

> I wanted to impress her,
> to make her think that I was something special:
> "Poor as the province was I got assigned to,"
> I told them both, "that doesn't mean I couldn't
> buy a fine team of eight upstanding porters."   [16–20]

Not quite a lie, but at some distance from the truth, as he rue-
fully admits:

> Needless to say, I nowhere own a single
> slave who'd be even capable of hoisting
> the whacked-off leg of some old beggar's pallet.
> True sluttishness will out. The harlot begged me,
> "Catullus, sweetie, lend 'em for an hour,
> I wanna worship at Serapis' temple."
> "Hold on," I told her, "when I said that I owned
> them, that I owned those slaves, I wasn't thinking—
> a dear friend of mine, Gaius, Gaius Cinna,
> he owns them, but although they're his, he lets me
> take them as though they were my own," I told her.
> "But really, there are some things I just can't take;
> tedious, tasteless, and insistent bitches
> with which you can't be off your guard one minute!"
>   [21–34]

The wit and attractiveness that Catullus saw in Varus' girlfriend at the beginning of the poem are canceled out by the
excessive literalness he discovers in her at the end.

In poem 10, the dialogue is clearly necessary: if we had

only the concluding excoriation, we would not be able to tell why Catullus was so angry with Varus' new flame. In its conclusion of such an extensive dialogue, however, the poem is very much an exception to Catullus' ordinary practice. Typically his poems begin with the invitation or excoriation, the Catullan moment, always in the present verging on the future. If the poem does not include or allude to the dialogue from which it emerged, then the poem in a sense has no past. That absence of a past and openness to the present typify Catullus' poems and seem to make them and him our contemporaries.

The idea of the dialogue also includes those situations in which its constituent conversations took place; when and where they occurred, who else was present at the time, what was said or could not be said, and what the motives of the speakers were. Those things were of no little interest to Catullus, as in poem 51 where he annotates, with an oddly detached precision, the auras and arrangements of one such occasion:

> To me that man seems like a god in heaven,
> seems—may I say it?—greater than all gods are,
> who sits by you and without interruption
>   watches you, listens
>
> to your sweet laughter, which casts such confusion
> onto my senses, Lesbia, that when I
> gaze at you merely, all of my well-chosen
>   words are forgotten
>
> as my tongue thickens and a subtle fire
> runs through my body while my ears are deafened
> by their own ringing and at once my eyes are
>   covered in darkness   [1–12]

The first three stanzas of poem 51 construct an ironic and unequal triangle between Lesbia, her current *amant en titre* who sits facing her, and Catullus, who also faces Lesbia but not directly and from some distance. This is not explicitly a poem-as-invitation, but one in which the desire for an invitation is everywhere apparent. In poem 51, there is no dialogue between Catullus and Lesbia; instead, there is her dialogue with another man, and Catullus' own craving for similar discourse, a desire so intense that it paradoxically results in his speechlessness. The absence of dialogue supports the notion that this was the first poem Catullus wrote to Lesbia.

Elsewhere Catullus shows his acute understanding of how utterance is explicable only in its context and how context can never be understood without reference to the often contradictory subtending of motive, as in poem 83:

> Lesbia hurls abuse at me in front of her husband:
>> that fatuous person finds it highly amusing!
> Nothing gets through to you, jackass—for silence would signal
>> that she'd been cured of me, but her barking and bitching
> show that not only haven't I not been forgotten,
>> but that this burns her: and so she rants and rages.
>
>   [1–6]

The Catullan poem does not emerge from primordial silence into language; rather, it interrupts the conversations that surround it, and in some instances, as here, it seizes on previous dialogue to fashion itself. This poem requires at least two conversations, the first, between Lesbia and her husband, in which she badmouths Catullus. But since it is highly unlikely that either of them would have passed this information on to Catullus, and since he was apparently not present during her harangue, we have to assume the presence of a third party—another hopeful lover, perhaps—who gleefully conveyed the bad news to the poet in a second conversation.

Not all of the poems are addressed to others, and two in which Catullus addresses himself show an interesting variation on the dialogue-invitation format of poem 10.

Poem 8 was apparently written when Catullus realized

that there would be no reconciliation with Lesbia. It begins
with an interior voice addressing Catullus, the voice of an em-
inently sensible comforter in a time of great trouble. Catullus
must recognize that it is all over, the voice tells him; he must
turn his back on what he and his mistress once had together,
and harden himself against her influence:

A Miser Catulle, desinas ineptire,
  et quod vides perisse perditum ducas.

 Fulsere quondam candidi tibi soles,
 cum ventitabas quo puella ducebat
B amata nobis quantum amabitur nulla.
 ibi illa multa tum iocosa fiebant,
 quae tu volebas nec puella nolebat.
 fulsere vere candidi tibi soles.

C nunc iam illa non vult: tu quoque, impotens, noli,
 nec quae fugit sectare, nec miser vive,
 sed obstinata mente perfer, obdura.

A Wretched Catullus! You have to stop this nonsense,
 admit that what you see has ended is over!

 Once there were days which shone for you with rare
   brightness,
 when you would follow wherever your lady led you,
 the one we once loved as we will love no other;
B there was no end in those days to our pleasures,
 when what you wished for was what she also wanted.
 Yes, there were days which shone for you with rare
   brightness.

 Now she no longer wishes; you mustn't want it,
C you've got to stop chasing her now—cut your losses,
 harden your heart and hold out firmly against her.
           [1–11]

This portion of the poem can be divided into three parts, A,
B, and C. The A and C portions each consist of a single sentence, and the premise advanced in A is supported by the con-

clusion drawn in C: this is the situation, recognize it, here's what you ought to do. But the B section sounds a contrasting theme. The comforter's sensible voice continues to address Catullus in the second person, but the melancholy recollection of the lovers' shared past strains against the good advice offered. If the purpose of the section is to demonstrate the great loss of surrendering the mistress, it also seems to show a certain weakening of resolve, a yearning for the return of those days of radiant unanimity. No, answers that same voice emphatically, *"nunc iam illa non vult."* The inner voice of good sense proceeds to tell Catullus precisely what he must do. The poem then is a meditation in the form of an internal dialogue between good sense urging its necessary course and unrelenting passion trying to relive its happiest moments, perhaps to make those moments come again. This section of the poem corresponds to the dialogue in poem 10; that dialogue over, the poem then moves into the negative invitation, the dismissal of the lady:

    Vale, puella! iam Catullus obdurat,
A nec te requiret nec rogabit invitam:
    at tu dolebis, cum rogaberis nulla.

    Scelesta, vae te! quae tibi manet vita!
B quis nunc te adibit? cui videberis bella?
    quem nunc amabis? cuius esse diceris?
    quem basiabis? cui labella mordebis?

C at tu Catulle, destinatus obdura.

    Goodbye now, lady! Catullus' heart is hardened,
A he will not look to you nor call against your wishes—
    how you'll regret it when nobody comes calling!

    so much for you, bitch—your life is all behind you!
B Now who will come to see you, thinking you lovely?
    whom will you love now, and whom will you belong to?
    whom will you kiss? and whose lips will you nibble?

C But you, Catullus! You must hold out now, firmly!

                                 [12–19]

Although shorter than the first section of the poem, this section can also be divided into three parts related by voice and sentiment to the corresponding parts of the first section.

Catullus now begins to speak for himself, apparently convinced by the voice of good sense. He echoes the hard line of the wisdom offered in A and C, returning its emphatic *obdura* in line 11 with his own no less emphatic *obdurat* in line 12. And yet, if he has been persuaded to follow this good advice, why does he speak of himself in the third person rather than in the second, as he does in other poems? The irresolute doubling continues here, as though Catullus were borrowing the forcefulness of that other voice to conceal the weakness of his own. He continues in this voice in part B, in contrast to the earlier B section when Lesbia was loved as no one else ever will be. Those words will be given an ironic twist in the second part of the poem, for in the future she will be loved by no one. The long, lyrical sentences that described their shared past are now contrasted with lines broken up by syntactical caesuras into short, choppy sentences. She will perhaps recall those days of radiant unanimity, those past intimacies that he now flings in her face as she dwindles away, alone and unloved.

And yet. Just as the first B passage contrasted with the A and C passages, so this later B section reveals an increasing irresolution in Catullus' part, as the fate he predicts for the woman leads him to recall their own physical intimacies with a vividness that can only weaken his resolve. Is he not in danger of wavering from his fixed purpose here? Perhaps that is why the voice of good sense returns with the last word, addressing Catullus as before in the second person—*at tu, Catulle*—to remind Catullus of his resolve and caution him to steadfastness.

A complicated polyphony: the A and C passages of each section support one another, and the B passages contrast not only with A and C but also with each other in their description of past and future, and yet agreeing in their irresolution.

Is this the work of a spontaneous songbird or a cerebral Alexandrian? The poem is also full of intriguing echoes and

repetitions, on which I have barely touched. In the first B passage the evocative *desinas* of the opening line is echoed in the
destinatus of the last; the *obdura* that ends the first part of the
poem also concludes the second. And, in the last line, the delicate, almost absent-minded rhyme of *at tu* with *Catulle* reminds us of another *at tu* in the poem: *at tu dolebis*, "But you
will grieve." Who will?

Surely he means the woman to whom he gave the false
name which appears concealed as an anagram in the verb chosen by that cerebral songbird, that spontaneous Alexandrian:
dolebis = Lesbi . . . Ah.

The voices of that poem lead its maker back and forth before ending on the note of requisite obduracy. Poem 76 offers
another version of an interior monologue illustrating the dialogue-invitation format. (Interestingly, though the poems are
of different length, the proportion of lines of dialogue and invitation in both poems is nearly identical.) Once again the
poem involves the poet's apparently insoluble problems with
Lesbia, but here, though still tormented, Catullus has clearly
recognized that only a total break with Lesbia offers him a way
out. His heightened sense of resolution is reflected in the more
straightforward structure of this poem, a dialogue for two
voices in succession. The first voice rehearses the poet's side
of his previous dialogue with Lesbia:

> If any pleasure can come to a man through recalling
>   decent behavior in his relations with others,
> not breaking his word, and never, in any agreement,
>   deceiving men by abusing vows sworn to heaven,
> then countless joys will await you in old age, Catullus,
>   as a reward for this unrequited passion!
> For all of those things which a man could possibly
>   say or
>   do have all been said and done by you already,
> and none of them counted for anything, thanks to her
>   vileness.
>   Then why endure your self-torment any longer?

why not abandon this wretched affair altogether,
 spare yourself pain the gods don't intend you to
  suffer?
It's hard to break off with someone you've loved for
 such a long time:
 it's hard, but you have to do it, somehow or other.
your only chance is to get out from under this sickness
 no matter whether or not you think you're able.
             [1–16]

The second voice then responds with a prayer, an invitation to
the gods to deliver him from his obsessive torment:

O gods, if pity is yours, or if ever to any
 who lay near death you offered the gift of your mercy,
look on my suffering: if my life seems to you decent,
 then tear from within me this devouring cancer,
this heavy dullness wasting the joints of my body,
 completely driving every joy from my spirit!
Now I no longer ask that she love me as I love her,
 or—even less likely—that she give up the others:
all that I ask for is health, an end to this foul sickness!
 O gods, grant me this in exchange for my devotion.
             [17–26]

Poem 51 is often taken as the first poem that Catullus wrote
to Lesbia, and it could have been, but what was the last poem?
Poem 11 is frequently mentioned as a contender, but surely the
savagery of its attack on her as well as its self-pitying, self-
immolating conclusion invite a response, as does poem 8 with
its contrasting evocations of past and future. Only in poem 76
does the poet realize that the only solution is silence on his
part, an end to the dialogue between them: silence would
mean that he had been cured of his *taetrum morbum*, his foul
sickness. The second voice of that poem does not address Lesbia, though of course she may be presumed to overhear its petition to heaven. This plea for a kind of justice not usually

associated with love affairs is as clear an indication as any that the dialogue is indeed over.

The Catullan moment is the moment of invitation, an instant poised between the past and future of a relationship, when whatever spatial or emotional distance there may have been between Catullus and the recipient of the poem suddenly collapses under the urgent pressure of direct address: *Vivamus, mea Lesbia, atque amemus!* The past dialogue between Catullus and Lesbia is canceled with that invitation. Not only whatever of the past they have shared together, but, it would seem, the past entirely; for, in the light of that sudden erotic summons, all of the stored up wisdom of the ages can be reduced to the censorious chattering of old men, before it is dismissed altogether as worthless:

> and let us value at a single penny
> all the loose flap of senile busybodies!   [2–3]

What truly matters is only what will happen from this point on in the relationship; the poem has no memory of the dialogue that preceded it.

The moment of the invitation precedes the experience to which it refers. That experience may be seen as an event or an occasion: a busy afternoon spent with Ipsitilla or a dinner party given for Fabullus. Or the experience may be seen as an alteration in an existing relationship, as in poem 5. But these are really just two ways of looking at the same phenomenon: the most important characteristic of these poems is that they are about something that has not yet happened or does not yet exist.

What then are these poems about? Often they are about themselves. One line of the modernist tradition in poetry emphasizes the self-referentiality of the work of art: Wallace Stevens' "poem of the mind in the act of finding / What will suffice."[10] In poems 8 and 76 we have seen Catullus' version of that kind of poem. There are others, such as poem 13:

Cenabis bene, mi Fabulle, apud me
paucis, si tibi di favent, diebus,
si tecum attuleris bonam atque magnam
cenam, non sine candida puella
et vino et sale et omnibus cachinnis.
Haec si, inquam, attuleris, venuste noster,
cenabis bene; nam tui Catulli
plenus sacculus est aranearum.

You will dine well with me, my dear Fabullus,
in a few days or so, the gods permitting.
Provided you provide the many-splendored
feast and invite your fair-complected lady,
your wine, your salt, and all the entertainment!
Which is to say, my dear, if you bring dinner,
you will dine well, for these days your Catullus
finds that his purse is only full of cobwebs.

Once again, the invitation refers to an event that has not yet
taken place, a happening that has not yet happened: a dinner
that Catullus will offer to Fabullus in the near future, but a
dinner so hedged about with conditions that we may assume
that Fabullus never reclined to enjoy it. The first line of the
poem confidently snaps out the offer, name of guest, where
held:

| *cenabis bene* | *mi Fabulle* | *apud me* |
| you will dine well | my Fabullus | at my place |

So far, so good: but the second line immediately proposes a
minor, if irritating, delay:

| *paucis* | *si tibi di favent* | *diebus* |
| in a few | (if the gods approve) | days |

Even if we admit that the conditional clause is a verbal equivalent to our custom of knocking on wood, it is hard to overlook
the fact that *paucis* is separated from *diebus* by nothing less than
the need for heaven's blessing on the enterprise: how odd that
an event as inconsequential as a dinner between two friends

should require such a prologue. But in the clever enjambment
at the end of the third line we see where the real problem lies:

> si tecum attuleris bonam atque magnam
> cenam

> Provided you provide the many-splendored
> feast

The dinner itself must be provided, and not only the dinner, for as subsequent lines reveal, Fabullus must provide a
girlfriend for the occasion, not to mention the wine, the salt,
and whatever entertainment he wishes. If we were to try to
specify the "subject" of this poem, we would conclude that
this is a poem about the impossibility of offering Fabullus an
invitation to dinner disguised as a poem offering Fabullus precisely that invitation.

Since the poem-as-invitation is about something that has
not yet happened—in this case, a dinner that isn't, apparently,
going to happen—it has another freedom that we associate
with modernism: it has no responsibility to depict things as
they are. This notion that the poet is free to make things up to
suit his purpose would not have been commonly accepted in
Catullus' day: it flew in the face of the Aristotelian defense of
poetry as a faithful representation of reality, or *mimesis*. Yet the
idea that the poet could make things up, could create monsters
of his own imagining, was very much in the air. It is an idea
which would have had much in it to recommend to Catullus,
who seems to be arguing a similar point in poem 16. If the
purpose of one kind of poetry is to excite lethargic libidos, a
certain amount of exaggeration, as in *milia basia* (thousands of
kisses), is not only necessary but desirable. And of course the
poem-as-invitation is intended, pace Auden, to make something happen. How it goes about doing this is very much its
own business, but neither monsters nor monstrous exaggerations may be excluded from its armory.

Because the poem-as-invitation always addresses someone and emerges from a dialogue with that person, the nature

of the recipient to a great extent determines the nature of the poem. One simply does not send the same kind of invitation to Ipsitilla that one sends to Lesbia, nor will these two women receive the same kind of invitation as our dear Fabullus. Nor, for that matter, can one send Lesbia the same invitation tomorrow that one might send her today, for relationships are in constant flux, and by tomorrow the desire to invite Lesbia to a lifetime of mutual bliss may be superseded by the need for a dismissive excoriation.

If the poem-as-invitation is specific to both its recipient and its occasion, then we have an explanation of the problem of Catullan variety, the great differences in tone and sentiment in the short poems that led Kenneth Quinn to formulate the notion of "levels of intent." For the apparent variety of the poems cannot be charged to the poet who made them; that variety is in the recipients and the occasions of the poems. And so, if we were to accuse Catullus of indecency in the poem to Ipsitilla, his response (were he able to respond) might be that it was Ipsitilla's fault, not his, for the poem he wrote to her was in fact tailored to the character of its recipient. Ipsitilla might be indecent and the poem he wrote for her might also be indecent, but their indecency cannot be projected back onto the poet: he was only observing a decorum proper to the recipient and the occasion.

This appears to be exactly what Catullus is saying in poem 16, when he responds to the charge of indecency brought against him by Furius and Aurelius:

> Purity's proper in the godly poet,
> but it's unnecessary in his verses.   [5–6]

Here Catullus projects the sexuality that others have found in his work onto the verses themselves and makes a clear distinction between himself and them. The verses may—in fact, as he says, they should—stir people up, but their attitudes cannot be imputed to him.

The poems then have a certain autonomy, a willfulness all

their own. The poet is only partially responsible for their actions. He may send one off to invite a guest to visit him at
Verona, as in poem 35, or send another off to insult an enemy,
as in poem 42. On the other hand, he may in fact be as much
the victim of the poems' excesses as the cause, considering the
odd notions that Furius and Aurelius seem to have gotten
about the poet's masculinity from reading his verses. Given
the satirical violence of so many of the poems, an element of
self-defense is no doubt involved. It seems equally true, however, that the specificity of the poems—their unique relation
to their recipients and to their occasions—confer upon them a
remarkable autonomy, a built-in defense against most kinds of
literary criticism, including the kind that would attempt to sort
the poems out according to their perceived "levels of intent."
For by what criteria can we judge poem 5 to be more "poetic"
than poem 32? Decorum rules, and the recipient of the poem
gets what he or she deserves. It could hardly be otherwise.

The poems derive another defense from their function as
invitations. Because the experience Catullus is writing about
has not yet happened and can only be anticipated, the audience for the poem can either (and only) be the recipient of the
invitation or the eavesdropper who overhears its delivery to
the recipient. We must include ourselves as bystanders, for as
readers we cannot be disinterested spectators evaluating a
work of art; we are in fact involved in the process of the poem,
as partisans, as helpful instruments of persuasion. When we
read Catullus' stirring evocation to his own hendecasyllabic
verses in poem 42, we are not intended to analyze that poem
for its pleasing symmetries. We can do so, just as we can analyze the structure of poem 8, given the leisure and the incli-
nation, but our main task is to cheer the verses on as they go
about theirs, and by our approval, to provide the poet with a
little extra muscle in this already uneven contest.

That being the case, how are we to evaluate these poems,
when they themselves seem to argue against the possibility of
our doing any such thing? This is not a problem that we would
have with Horace, for the act of memorializing experience

turns the reader of the poem into posterity, and it is the business of posterity to make judgments, to confer greatness upon the poem or condemn it to oblivion. But there is no place for posterity in the reception of a Catullan poem: because the experience he is writing about has not yet happened, the audience consists only of its recipient and those who (like ourselves) overhear the conversation between the poet and the recipient: there are no other possibilities. Just as Horace's audience can only consist of posterity, Catullus' audience can only consist of contemporaries, and that, of course, is another reason why his poems seem so modern to us.

The poems are noteworthy, if not notorious, for the lapel-grabbing abruptness with which they begin, thrusting themselves into pauses in the dialogue, forestalling at least for the moment any interruption from those they address. They summon us to attention with their commands, questions, promises, and threats; they try to be irresistible at the onset, as though they realize only too well how little time they have to make their case in the press of competing desires.

But the poems are also noteworthy for their conclusions, or more accurately for the ways they avoid conclusions. A number of poems end with a repetition of the line with which they begin, but this kind of ending is not a conclusion at all. Rather, it affirms the premise that began the poem and makes a simple point: no change. The situation that generated the poem in the first place still obtains at its end.

The conclusion to a poem releases us from the state of tension its accumulated energies generate and separates us from the experience the poem describes. In Horace's ode, the anxiety of the poet's imagined renewal of his relationship with Pyrrha is settled by the votive offering to Neptune. That account is now closed, the poet can rest, and his readers can learn how to manage their affairs by seeing how he has managed his: the notion is that we may indeed learn from our experiences.

But if we look in Catullus for a conclusion that offers us

the consolation that we can generalize from our past experience to safely navigate the Scylla and Charybdis of future doings, we will not find it. We come close to such a conclusion in poem 22, however, where Catullus denounces Suffenus for the man's vanity about his verses. In the last lines, Catullus moves from the specific to the general, citing a moral from Aesop:

> Conceited? yes, but show me a man who isn't:
> find someone who isn't like Suffenus in something.
> A glaring fault? It must be somebody else's:
> I carry mine in my backpack and ignore them. [18–21]

While this is a generalization, it would be a risky one to use as a guide to future experience, since it advises against making such judgments, all of us being equally fallible. In its last line, it also argues against the possibility of our ever having adequate knowledge of our faults.

But if Catullus' poems avoid formal conclusions they have good reasons for doing so, given the nature of the poem-as-invitation, which depends on the recipient for its conclusion, since an invitation is incomplete until answered. As persuasively as it can, the poem-as-invitation projects its needs, its wishes, its desires into the future, and then stops, expectantly. Only a response from outside the poem can complete it: the poem cannot plausibly answer the question it poses. That the poems are unfinished until answered accounts for the sense that readers have of them as fragmentary. We are used to the kind of conclusion that we find in Horace's poem, one that will release us from its concerns and restore us to ours. But the Catullan poem-as-invitation refuses to let us go at the end.

It is in closure that his poems are most vulnerable and most revealing; in the ending of poem 32, in fact, we have a literal case of self-exposure. Proper conclusions would release these poems from their anxiety. Instead, they conclude by generating fresh spasms of anxiety, urgencies which they hope to pass on to their recipients in the form of pleas, wishes, demands, threats, promises, and insults, all of which require some kind of answer. And only that response from beyond the poet's control and the boundaries of his poem can conclude it.

No conclusions, then. But from this inconclusiveness, certain conclusions may be drawn. Experience teaches Horace that he can learn from experience, that he can transcend it by memorializing it, turning it into a souvenir; experience teaches Catullus that he cannot learn from experience. The poem-as-invitation is a response to this knowledge.

Reality is unpredictable: a cherished brother dies; the woman, whom he loved as no one else ever will be loved, betrays him for another and another; close friends fall away. The social world seems to be a kaleidoscope of ever-changing loyalties, with self-interest the only constant. Catullus wrote many poems that Caesar is said to have said were permanently damaging to his reputation, yet Caesar invited Catullus to dinner one evening, and Catullus went.

Undoubtedly there are limitations to the Catullan poem-as-invitation: its frequent suppression of the past, its priority and purposiveness, its dependence on another person and a specific occasion, and, perhaps most important, its inability to transcend the limitations of particular experience and draw conclusions. These clearly are the poems of a self under siege. And yet, those limitations of its dependent, provisional nature offer Catullus a useful strategy for dealing with the reality of social life in his time.

Even as he searches to ground his existence in a foundation other than self-interest, the highly mobile poem-as-invitation allows him to keep his options open. His frequent suppression of the past leaves him open to the present and allows him to respond to love or betrayal with a unique vulnerability and directness. No doubt there were disadvantages to this poetic amnesia: if we cannot prepare ourselves for the shock of the future, the future is always going to shock us. But for his readers at least, the compensation comes with his openness to surprises, pleasurable and otherwise: Veranius returns unexpectedly from Spain, and Catullus celebrates the event in poem 9 with lines of uncomplicated joy; Rufus violates his trust, and Catullus responds with lines that conjure up the violence of anal rape.

The provisionality and mobility of the poem-as-invitation allow Catullus to engage the world in a state like that which a poet writing in English long after him described as "negative capability."

VI TRANSFORMATIONS OF THE GIFT

Ecstasy affords the occasion and expediency determines
the means.
—Marianne Moore

SURROUNDING THE RELATIVELY FEW POEMS TO OR ABOUT LESBIA
in the Book of Catullus are many others that have nothing to
do with her. Most of the polymetric poems fall into this category; consequently, they tend to be neglected in favor of the
Lesbia poems, which represent the essential Catullus for most
of his contemporary audience, whether classical scholar or
common reader. This is not entirely a modern notion, it would
seem: only a generation after Catullus, the poet Propertius
wrote of "Lesbia, who is even more famous than Helen."[1]

In addition to the absence of Lesbia, the poems suffer
from other perceived drawbacks, at least as far as sustained
critical attention is concerned: they are frequently comic and
not infrequently obscene. Comedy itself may be a serious subject for criticism, but surely these brief, often indecent jokes
are unworthy of serious consideration. And while Catullus' obscenity has always been of considerable interest to his readers,
few critics seem able, even today, to discuss the matter ratio-
nally. One often sympathizes: Catullan obscenity, in the vir-
ulence of its feeling and in the specificity of its detail, is equally
resistant to paraphrase and exegesis. It is easier to ignore it
altogether, or to argue that Catullus isn't really saying what he
seems to be saying, or to treat it as the manifestation of a (temporarily) pathological sensibility, than it is to see it as a necessary element of his poetic strategy. Even more troublesome
than the blatantly obscene poems are the tender, sentimental,
and amusing ones written to the youth Juventius, which raise

the issue of the poet's homoerotic attachment to a young boy, an issue many critics would prefer to ignore.

More damaging, perhaps, is that many of these poems seem defiantly casual in their openness to experience; if we were to alter the terms of Marianne Moore's famous aphorism to fit them, we would say that here opportunity affords the occasion. The poet seems willing to let circumstances provide him with subjects: a chance encounter with Varus in the forum leads to an unpleasant revelation about his friend's new mistress; dear Veranius returns unexpectedly from Spain and must be greeted with a poem; a dinner companion makes off with the poet's treasured napkin and has to be reminded that such activities are likely to bring swift poetic retribution. What is most striking about these poems is how very little Catullus needs to be moved to write them: the merest scrap of experience, the faintest stirring of the well will do it. Minor occasions, minor verse: Catullus develops them not as grains of sand in which eternity can be glimpsed but as incidental occurrences that reveal the dailiness of life.

These are minor poems, distinguished for levity, brevity, obscenity, and the casualness of their inspiration; the notion that they could be of considerable importance in the work of Catullus would not garner a great deal of support these days. Yet these poems are very much worthy of our critical attention. I believe that many of them represent a deliberate attempt by Catullus, perhaps rising to a challenge from Philodemus, to write an important poem made up of unimportant parts: minor poems that would explore a major theme: what is the relation between manners and morals, or, how should men behave in society?

Poem 1, the dedication to Cornelius Nepos, is not simply personal, but programmatic: its opening phrase, *Cui dono*, "To whom will I give," introduces the theme of gift-giving, which is closely related to the double-edged strategy of invitation and excoriation that we examined in chapter V. The *cui dono* poems treat their theme not in a static or systematic way but by following it through a series of transformations in which

the exchange of gifts and favors is emblematic of conviviality
itself and as related to morality as to manners. In this chapter
we shall consider the theme of the gift and its transformations,
chiefly, though not exclusively, in the polymetric poems.

For Catullus, the journey to the province of Bithynia,
where he would encounter his brother's troubled spirit for the
last time, must have seemed like a descent into the underworld. Troy was located in the province of Bithynia, and in
poem 68 Catullus identifies the mythic slaughter of the Trojan
War with his brother's death:

> damned Troy! The burial pit both of Europe and Asia,
>   untimely grave of heroes and heroic actions!
> Wasn't it Troy which brought sorrowful death to my
>   brother?   [89–91]

No wonder the homecoming from Bithynia afforded him such
an ecstatic occasion; in poem 4 we see the poet surrounded by
his friends, presiding over a poetic celebration of the yacht that
safely restored him to Italy and to their company:

> Closer, friends: this little yacht you see before you
> says that in her day no ship afloat was swifter,
> no craft cut water whose wake she wasn't able
> to leave behind, no matter whether her oarblades
> drove her along or she relied on her canvas!
> The shoreline of the blustery Adriatic
> won't deny it, nor will the Cycladic Islands,
> nor glamourous Rhodes, no—not even the wild Thracian
> Sea of Marmora, nor the grim gulf of Pontus,
> where in the past our future yacht resided
> as a green forest on the heights of Cytorus,
> and where she learned to lisp in leafy syllables.
> Pontic Amastrys, Cytorus of the boxwood,
> this little bean pod says that her past and present
> are well known to you; she's certain you remember
> how life began for her, perched atop your summit,

and how she first dipped her new oars into your waters,
leaving you on her maiden voyage through stormy
seas with her master, heading straight as an arrow
no matter whether the wind was holding steady
from port or starboard or from both sides together.
Nor was it ever necessary to offer
vows to the gods because of her performance
on the open seas and these more tranquil waters.
Now her career is ended, and in her old age
retiring, she dedicates herself to you two,
Castor the twin and the twin brother of Castor. [1–27]

The homecoming is an occasion to which he returns often in
these poems, sometimes to reflect with pleasure on his deliverance from bondage in Bithynia, and sometimes with rue to
recall the hardships he claims to have endured, quite literally,
under Memmius.

If the journey to Bithynia was a venture into the underworld, the return home is a return to life, and there could be
no better symbol of that return than the yacht that brings him
back to the waters of Lago di Garda, the *phasellus*. Romans
used that word figuratively to refer to small, seaworthy pleasure craft: its real meaning was "bean pod," and just as a real
bean pod shelters, nurtures, and delivers the life it contains,
likewise the nautical one.

The homecoming restores a lost member to the social
body, and so it requires a public celebration no less compelling
than the observance of grief. The rites involve the offering of
a gift to Castor and Pollux, the twin gods charged with pro-
tecting seafarers.

But gifts are not only given to the gods, and the importance of gift-giving as one of the indispensable rites of civilized
beings is a theme announced in the question with which the
Book of Catullus begins:

To whom will I give this sophisticated,
abrasively accomplished new collection?

This is a particular kind of book, distinguished for its cleverness and its modernity: it is not for everyone, for not everyone
will approve of it, and so it cannot be dedicated to just anyone.
The poet must select the appropriate recipient on the basis of
compatibility and cultural distinction:

> To you, Cornelius! you had the habit
> of making much of my poetic little,
> when you, the first in Italy, were boldly
> unfolding all past ages in three volumes,
> a monument of scholarship and labor!

Because of his support of Catullus' poetic ambitions and his
own accomplishment as a historian, Nepos is the perfect recipient of this gift, and his acceptance of the book, however
unworthy it is of his attentions, will transform the item; distinguished now by the distinguished patron's acceptance, the
book may appropriately seek, if not immortality, at least longevity:

> And so it's yours; I hand this slim book over,
> such as it is—for the sake of its patron
> may it survive a century or better.

The last transformation is an implicit one, as the gift of the
book, once offered and accepted, must strengthen the relationship between Nepos and Catullus.

Directly after poem 2 come three lines that do not seem
to belong to that poem; these verses may have originally been
connected to the fragment that comes after poem 14, or they
may have been part of a poem that is now missing. At any rate,
they also play with the theme of gift-giving:

> I'd be as pleased by that as Atalanta
> was, in the story, with the golden apple
> that freed her of virginity's restrictions.   [2b, 1–3]

Catullus refers to the gift of a golden apple, a present from
Aphrodite to Atalanta's suitor, Hippomenes, who tossed it at
her feet in order to beguile them from the race course. Having

lost the race, Atalanta was forced to accept Hippomenes as her
husband, exchanging her virginity for the golden apple. For
Catullus, the gift of an apple is linked to the idea of erotic fulfillment: the reader will recall another situation concerning an
apple, a maiden, and a suitor in poem 65.

Poem 4 subtly reiterates the theme of poem 1 with a different gift, a different kind of dedication. In both poems, the
gift is not in itself of great value. Catullus speaks of the book
he offers Nepos in disparaging terms: "I hand this slim book
over, / such as it is." In its own right, it hardly merits immortality, but with the luster from its association with Nepos, who
will cherish it because of *his* association with Catullus, it may
endure. Similarly, the vessel that Catullus offers the Dioscuri
may appear to be nothing more than a *phasellus*, a sea-going
bean pod, but those who know the story of its unrivaled
speed, its lofty origins, and life of distinguished service, not
to mention its success in bringing its grateful master back to
the shores of Italy, will cherish it not so much for what it is—
a bean pod—but rather for what it represents to the poet.

The gift as a locus of emotionally resonant associations is
the subject of many of these poems, including the appealing
trio of poems 12, 13, and 14. Poem 12 is addressed to one Marrucinus Asinius:

> It's sinister, Asinius—your practice
> of lifting our unprotected napkins
> while we're all deep in wine and conversation!
> You're crazy if you think you're being clever:
> what could be shabbier or less attractive?
> But don't take my word—go and ask your brother,
> for Pollio would gladly spend a fortune
> to keep it quiet; that boy is a master
> of every grace that's charming and delightful.
> So, either send me back my linen napkin
> or else expect three hundred savage verses—
> I'm not upset because it was expensive,

but it's a gift which calls to mind a friendship:
Veranius and my Fabullus sent it
all the way back from Spain for me, a present
which I must therefore cherish as I cherish
my dear Fabullus and Veraniolus.   [1–17]

Not until near the end of this poem do we learn the cause of
the poet's anger: the napkin was a gift from his friends. It is
treasured not for itself but because it calls to mind a friendship.

The poem is actually a tissue of complicated exchanges:
the loving gift of Veranius and Fabullus to Catullus has been
stolen by someone who is as blind to its worth as to the sig-
nificance and consequences of his actions. The thief's brother
sees the reality—one gets the impression that this is his
habit—and offers another exchange: he would be willing to
buy silence with his own money. But that gambit is declined,
and the poet proposes an exchange of his own: either the napkin will be returned, or swift and certain retribution will follow—three hundred hendecasyllabic verses. Here we may see
the true value of the napkin in Catullus' eyes: in a society
where a couplet could destroy a reputation, three hundred
verses would represent what the military refer to as "redun-
dancy."

Poem 12 ends with mention of the poet's friend Fabullus,
and poem 13 begins by addressing him directly:

You will dine well with me, my dear Fabullus,
in a few days or so, the gods permitting.
Provided you provide the many-splendored
feast and invite your fair-complected lady,
your wine, your salt, and all the entertainment!
Which is to say, my dear, if you bring dinner
you will dine well, for these days your Catullus
finds that his purse is only full of cobwebs.   [1–8]

If his poverty—no doubt temporary, and the consequence
perhaps of his trip to Bithynia—prevents him from offering
Fabullus a real dinner, the poet will demonstrate his own con-

viviality by offering Fabullus, in exchange for the dinner that
Fabullus must now provide, another gift:

> But in return, you'll have from me Love's Essence,
> or what (if anything) is more delicious:
> I'll let you sniff a certain charming fragrance
> which Venuses and Cupids gave my lady;
> one whiff of it, Fabullus, and you'll beg the
> gods to transform you into nose, completely!   [9–14]

Like the napkin Veranius and Fabullus gave Catullus, this gift
is treasured not for its financial worth (though, like napkins,
unguents were indeed expensive gifts) but for the value of its
associations. It also was a gift of love, given Catullus by his
puella, and she received it—so he claims—directly from Venus
and Cupid: no wonder then that nothing could be more elegant. Its erotic refinement makes it an appropriate gift for Fabullus, who shares that quality: he is addressed as *venuste
noster*, Venus' darling and ours, too. The implied identification of gift with recipient will become so obvious that Fabullus
will wish to identify with it completely, and will petition the
gods to be turned entirely into its servant. Like poem 12, poem
13 also presents us with a complicated series of exchanged
gifts; we begin with the gift of a dinner that Catullus offers
Fabullus which turns into a dinner Fabullus must offer Catullus; in exchange, Catullus will offer Fabullus a gift he received
from his puella, who had it in turn from Venus and Cupid.
The origin of this gift with the goddess of love and the transformation of its recipient recall fragment 2b, for the golden
apple was given to Hippomenes by Aphrodite. When he gave
it to Atalanta, she, like Fabullus, was transformed: betrayed by
her sexuality and paralyzed by the indecisiveness that cost her
the race.

Poem 13 ends with Fabullus' nose, and poem 14 begins
with Catullus' eyes:

> Calvus, you darling, if I didn't love you
> more than my own eyes, this gift would make me

> hate you as much as Vatinius hates you!
> What did I say or do to give you reason
> for wasting me with such outrageous poets?   [1–5]

Friends customarily exchanged gifts on the feast of the Sat-
urnalia, and the gift Calvus has sent Catullus is an anthology
of bad verse. There is an easy, yet elegant, antithesis in the
first three lines of the poem, which divide neatly between Catullus' protestations of his extraordinary affection for Calvus
and his equally vehement declaration of the outrageousness of
the gift (Vatinius and Calvus were mortal enemies). How could
Calvus have done such a thing? Interestingly, this gift also did
not originate with the giver: it had been given Calvus by someone else—by one of his clients, no doubt, in exchange for Calvus' legal labors on his behalf:

> But if—as I suspect—this rare, exquisite
> work is your fee from Sulla the schoolmaster,
> then it's another story: I'm delighted
> to learn that you got anything from *that* one!   [8–11]

Having settled the matter to his satisfaction, Catullus is still
left with the book on his hands and the need to repay Calvus
in kind. The only appropriate response is even more wretched
verse:

> How clever of you! But it isn't finished:
> if morning ever comes, I'll run and gather
> all sorts of poison from the bins of bookstalls:
> men like Suffenus, Caesius, Aquinus,
> abominations fit for retribution!
> —And, as for you, damned nuisances, you're banished;
> limp back on wretched feet to your creators,
> the worst of poets and the age's penance!   [16–23]

There are intriguing thematic and verbal repetitions, casually
rather than causally linking these poems and one that precedes them. Poem 10 ends with Catullus' charge against a new
girlfriend of Varus; she is one with whom one cannot be at

ease, *per quam non licet esse neglegentem*. Poem 12 begins with
Asinius, who carries off napkins when the company *is* at ease:
tollis lintea neglegentiorum. Poem 12 ends with a reference to
Fabullus, who is directly addressed at the beginning of poem
13. Poems 12, 13, and 14 deal with gifts, each linked to an appropriate part of the body: we pick up napkins with our fingers, unless we steal them from the unwary, in which case we
use our sinister left hand; napkins are to hands as unguents
are to noses, as our beloved eyes are to wretched books of poetry. Are we meant to see these devices as a way of forging
unity in diversity? Or were they perhaps the poet's responses
to the challenge of a poetic game?

The gifts are all items that would be appropriately brought
to, used, and exchanged at a *convivium*; in fact, conviviality or
its absence may be seen in the use or misuse of such gifts.
Napkins were socially necessary because at a Roman banquet
one ate with one's fingers. If Catullus' napkin has been stolen,
then he must face the company in embarrassment, with traces
of the meal on his fingers and lips. Unguents were also associated with such feasts. In an indulgent mood, Cicero describes Marcus Caelius Rufus as a young man who, it is said,
"never passed up a dinner invitation, who went to the gar-
dens, who used unguents, who was seen at Baiae."[2] Those
things, according to the censorious elders, all went together
and marked a young man as a rake on the way to ruin. Likewise, books of poetry, like Catullus' own books or like the Roman version of *The Stuffed Owl* presented him by Calvus, were
exchanged as gifts at dinner parties.

The gifts are not given carelessly or gratuitously. The moment when the gift is offered is privileged, extrapolated from
a complex social relationship between giver and recipient. That
relationship, the social context of the poem, surrounds it and
shapes its utterance. The gift in each case is emblematic of the
exchange characteristic of the relationship. Thus the book of
poems to Cornelius Nepos, in exchange for his once and no
doubt future encouragement of Catullus' poetic ambitions.

And thus the votive model of the phasellus to the Dioscuri, in exchange for the poet's safe deliverance from his perilous sea journey. Fabullus, who is *venuste noster*, is the appropriate recipient of a gift that originates with Venus, the source of erotic sensibility and charm. Likewise, such offerings are made at significant times: the moment of publication or the celebration of homecoming.

The value of the gift is not to be equated with its financial worth, although some of these gifts—the napkin, the unguent—were probably very expensive items. Rather, their value derives from the associations that surround them. Thus the napkin is valuable because it is emblematic of the love that Veranius and Fabullus have for Catullus and he for them, and the value of the unguent derives from its distinguished origins. The freely given gift may be passed on to others, and at each step it acquires more loving associations and becomes more precious. In the case of *The Stuffed Owl* of poem 12, a similar process obtains. Sulla the schoolmaster no doubt gave Calvus the anthology simply because it was a book of verse, and he knew that Calvus was a poet. Because he *was* a poet, Calvus knew how bad the book was and added the value of his own ironic intelligence to the gift when he passed it on to Catullus. The act of giving thus adds value to a gift in the form of consciousness, transforming the object into something of greater worth. If it were not emblematic of his friends' love, the napkin would be nothing more than a piece of expensive cloth. And the book that Catullus dedicates to Nepos will take on a new luster from its association with so distinguished a patron.

This accounts for Catullus' anger at theft, which strikes a blow at that trusting negligence which is the basis of all conviviality. Moreover, friendship and conviviality oblige one to give: to offer an unguent when one cannot give the dinner that should accompany it or give a translation of Callimachus when one cannot give an original poetic composition. Theft interrupts that chain of reciprocal exchanges. It also reveals the thief as socially inept, like Thallus, for instance, in poem 25:

Thallus, you fairy far far softer than the fur of bunny
or the down of goose or the fine fuzz of a fuzzy earlobe
or an old man's limp dick or the dusty cobwebs that it's
    hung with—
Thallus, who sweeps up our belongings like a crazed
    cyclone
when the goddess of sloth reveals that his victims are
    nodding—
send them *all* back to me: the cloak you've lately
    pounced upon and
my Spanish napkins and my notebooks full of Eastern
    sketches
which you (dumb booby) openly display—as family
    heirlooms!   [1–8]

The crime for which Thallus is abused is similar to that which
Asinius has committed, but Thallus' offense is the greater,
since he attempts to surround the stolen items with false associations of his own devising by passing them off as family
heirlooms. Oblivious of their real provenance, he assumes that
everyone else is likewise ignorant, but they aren't—or at least
they won't be, after this poem circulates—and Thallus will be
revealed for the appalling boor that he is.

    Silence poses another danger to conviviality, since, like
theft, it interrupts the natural exchange of gifts and represents
hoarding, keeping an experience to oneself rather than sharing
it with one's friends. This is not only unsociable but pointless,
at least when Catullus is nosing around for gossip. Those who
attempt to keep certain matters to themselves are likely to become the hapless objects of indecent speculation, like Flavius
in poem 6:

Flavius, if your new infatuation
weren't some dull slut, you wouldn't keep silent—
you'd *have* to tell Catullus all about her.
I really can't imagine this hot-blooded
whore you're so keen on—shame must have you
    tongue-tied!

You do not lie alone: even though speechless,
your little love nest is a revelation,
dripping with garlands and exotic odors,
not to mention the battered pillows scattered
around the couch gone prematurely feeble
from your incessant nighttime acrobatics!
There isn't any point to keeping quiet:
flabless from fucking, your attenuated
buttocks attest to your indecent doings!
So whatever you have, whether nice or nasty,
tell us—for I would raise you and your passion
right up to heaven with my clever verses.   [1–17]

Clearly, there is more to this poem than we are told. Catullus
and Flavius are friends, for Catullus implies that Flavius usually confides in him and would do so in this case if secrecy were
not so essential. If Flavius is Catullus' friend, then Catullus'
explanation for the secrecy, that Flavius must be a man of good
taste in these matters, is improbable at best. The reason for
secrecy must lie elsewhere: the woman no doubt has a jealous
husband or another lover. Catullus of course knows this but
playfully chooses to accuse Flavius of consorting with an un-
presentable slut in order to goad him into providing the juicy
gossip Catullus wants to hear. Poem 55, addressed to a friend
named Camerius, reveals a similar situation. Camerius has
been hiding out from his friends:

Tell us, if it isn't too much trouble,
where it is that you've been lurking lately.
We've looked all over for you—at the racetrack,
at the Circus, in the forum's bookstalls,
the sacred temple of great Jupiter!
I went as far as Pompey's portico,
questioning every hooker who approached me:
what a lot of innocent expressions!
Unconvinced, I finally exploded:
"Give me Camerius, you bargain baggage!"

One answered me with a complete disclosure:
"He's hiding here between my blushing titties." [1–12]

Like Flavius, Camerius is detained by a woman who keeps him
from his usual haunts. But here Catullus offers a reason for the
persistence of his inquiries:

If you remain obstinately tongue-tied,
the rewards of love will all escape you:
Venus loves nothing more than juicy gossip.
But if you must, keep it from the others,
so long as I can share your little secret!   [18–22]

The last two lines of the poem are clearly ironic, since we may
assume that once Catullus learned the details, they would be
a secret no longer: he would celebrate this affair in his verse,
just as he would celebrate that of Flavius. And so, what he is
offering Flavius in that earlier poem is the gift of poetry, his
clever verses that will immortalize the two lovers. In poem 1,
Catullus offers Nepos a book of poems in exchange for his earlier words of encouragement to the poet as well as for the
words in Nepos' three-volume universal history. In poem 6 he
offers Flavius a similar gift, poems that will immortalize him
and his beloved, in exchange for Flavius' words. By his mis-
guided and wholly unsuccessful attempts to conceal the affair,
Flavius is cheating Catullus, preventing him from completing
the social exchange by offering an appropriate gift. The fact
that the gift, if given, would be completely inappropriate, dev-
astating to the lovers' need for privacy, only makes the situation more amusing. If your friend is a poet, then one of the
obligations of friendship is to provide him with the occasions
of verse, no matter how inconvenient such occasions may be
to you.

The gift is transformed when given to another, and the
recipient is changed in turn. These transformations either in-
crease the vitality of the recipient or diminish it. After he receives the anthology of wretched verse, which he describes

as a malign force sent to destroy him, Catullus is—or at least pretends to be—transformed from a loving friend into a perishing victim in search of appropriate vengeance: in this case, venom gathered from the stalls of booksellers. In contrast, the most dramatic and significant of the transformations occurs when the gift of the unguent promised to Fabullus at the end of poem 13 clearly increases his vitality. It will so enchant him, not only by its aroma but also by its association with the goddess of love herself, that he will desire only to be transformed entirely to nose. That transformation is explicitly an erotic one; part of the reason why the poem is so funny is that we recognize, in the concentration of Fabullus' sensuality into a single, enlarged organ, an erection of the nose.

The gift transforms its recipient and is itself transformed—in the case of the unguent, it is to be consumed by use. But the unguent was given to Fabullus as a substitute for a dinner Catullus could not provide. And here we see that the transformation of both gift and recipient is emblematic of the essential exchange and transformation of the convivium itself, where the dinner that is consumed then restores and eroticizes the body of the recipient. Catullus describes that transformation explicitly in poem 32, when the lunch he has eaten turns the poet into an erect penis:

I beg of you, my sweet, my Ipsitilla,
my darling, my sophisticated beauty,
invite me over for an assignation;
and, if you're willing, do me one big favor:
don't let another client shoot the door bolt,
and don't decide to suddenly go cruising,
but stay at home and get yourself all ready
for nine—yes, nine—successive copulations!
Honestly, if you want it, give the order:
I've eaten, and I'm sated, supinated!
My prick is poking through my cloak and tunic. [1–11]

The relationship between dinner and desire could not be more explicitly rendered than in the last two lines of this poem,

where the gratification of one appetite instantly awakens another, which can only be satisfied by Ipsitilla or someone like
her. The body restored to life is a social body, and as in poem
4, it craves company.

The gifts, as we have seen, were inanimate objects that
transformed their recipient even as the objects themselves
were transformed by the act of gift-giving. This transformation
is emblematic of the restoration of physical vigor through the
act of eating. Eating is a paradoxical activity, for when we eat
we take death into our bodies by devouring what has been
slain or harvested, which miraculously sustains life within us.
We feast at a wake: in the presence of death, we take death
into ourselves in order to restore ourselves and the community
we are part of to life. And of course the traditional burial rites
for the Roman dead, like those that Catullus mentions in the
elegy for his brother, included gifts of food and flowers.

The paradoxical continuity between death, food, and desire, the ironies that link the cold and the calories, were noted
by Wallace Stevens in "The Emperor of Ice Cream":

> Call the roller of big cigars,
> The muscular one, and bid him whip
> In kitchen cups concupiscent curds.[3]

After the curds, Catullus would have agreed, comes the con-
cupiscence. That ironic connection between death, dinner,
and desire is also the subject of poem 59, a handful of lines
about a woman named Rufa:

RUFA THE BOLOGNESE WIFE OF MENENIUS
SUCKS OFF RUFULUS

> Often in some cheap graveyard
> you will have seen her snatch a loaf as it tumbles
> from the fiery logs of the funeral pyre,
> while taking her licks from the half-shaven corpse burner.

[1–5]

The poem begins with a curiously specific identification, as though Catullus were at some pains to make sure that we did not confuse this Rufa with any others. The act she is accused of in the first sentence is described with a bluntness that suggests that Catullus is either inscribing the charge on a wall or copying it from one.

For Catullus, fellatio is emblematic of sexual rapacity, the act of a prostitute whose poverty compels her to perform her services out-of-doors. In poem 58, where Catullus describes the degradation of Lesbia, he pictures her in those terms:

> nunc in quadriviis et angiportis
> glubit magnanimi Remi nepotes

> now on streetcorners and in wretched alleys
> she shucks the offspring of greathearted Remus. [4–5]

Here Lesbia is evidently preparing a client for fellatio; the verb *glubere* means to peel away bark or the rind of a fruit before eating. Lesbia's brother, Lesbius, in poem 79 shows a proclivity for this kind of activity that makes decent men avoid the traditional greeting among Roman men—a kiss on the lips—when they meet him. And of course Gellius is similarly inclined in poem 80, where Catullus links fellatio and eating:

> Gellius, what shall I tell them? They ask why your rosy
>   lips are much whiter than even the snows of winter,
> when you set out from home in the morning and when
>   you awaken
>   from your luxurious midafternoon siesta.
> I don't know for certain, but isn't it true what they
>   whisper:
> "The juicy fruit he favors
> comes in human flavors."
> It must be: poor Victor's blue balls blurt out your vile
>   secret
>   just as your lips do, stained with his strained-off
>   semen.   [1–8]

We see the same connection between eating men and eating food in the poem about Rufa: her poverty, if not her predilection, compels her to seek out nourishment in the only places where she can readily find it. She takes the vitality of Rufus in oral sex, and she supplements this diet by robbing the dead of the only vitality they have left, the loaves of bread that accompany them to the funeral pyre as afterlife offerings. She steals the loaves, scraps of life, from the fires of death, while the half-shaven corpse burner—this is clearly not the Forest Lawn of Roman cemeteries—has at her. The verb *tundere* means to beat or thump upon someone or something and has an explicitly sexual connotation, for as Rufa steals life from death, death's own attendant is banging away at her.

The connection between poverty, rapacity, and sexual voraciousness is also touched on in poem 33, where two bathhouse habitués, Vibennius and his apparently notorious son, are castigated for their crimes:

> O best of all who work the bathhouse rackets,
> Vibennius and Son—that letching asshole!
> (for father's hand is utterly rapacious
> and his boy's fanny is no less voracious)   [1–4]

Catullus represents the sexual rapacity of Vibennius' son as a voracious anus. Here the confusion between mouth and anus is made explicit by the word *vorax*, meaning voracious or gluttonous. Poverty, hunger, and sexual rapacity go hand in hand in these poems, and often rapacity manifests itself as a confusion between mouth and anus. Poem 97, for example, attacks Aemilius, and Catullus begins by mulling over what appears to be a matter of all-consuming interest:

> Really, I shouldn't have thought that it made any
>   difference
> whether Aemilius opened his mouth or his asshole:
> one wouldn't expect to find elegance wafting from
>   either.
> His asshole, however, *does* show greater refinement,
> since it has no teeth   [1–5]

But Catullus is not satisfied to end the discussion here and proceeds from Aemilus' teeth to a further comparison:

> His teeth are really enormous,
> set maladroitly in gums of saddlebag leather,
> and when (as he's wont to) he grins, one thinks of the gaping
> cunt of a she-mule in heat, pissing profusely.

Here we have a metaphoric confusion of orifices made even worse—if possible—by the nature of the beast to which the hapless Aemilius is compared. Finally, the man is so repellent that Catullus is almost at a loss to say how revolting a woman who slept with him would be:

> Surely the woman who went with him ought to take pleasure
> in licking clean a sickly old hangman's asshole. [11–12]

Once again, as in the lines about Rufa, death enters the poem—here in the form of the *carnifex*, the hangman and torturer. Copulating with Aemilius is the equivalent of eating one's way into the very bowels of death.

Giving such poems so dispassionate a reading is necessary if we are to see them as more than merely obscene jokes, but it is also necessary to underscore the pain and the sexual horror that underlies them. Catullus offers a nightmare as bleak as any modern comedian—a Beckett, a Celine—might imagine.

Against the background of the inelegant rapacity and crude violence of anal sex in bath houses and oral sex in alleyways appears the innocent interlude of the poet's relationship with the boy Juventius. In describing it as innocent, I do not deny that the relationship was an erotic one. Obviously it was that, but the poems to and about Juventius reveal the outline of a sentimental drama of adoring pursuit and unwavering resistance: that the chase should end in a sexual consummation seems not to have been all that devoutly desired, at least not by either of the principals involved.

Dinner turns into desire, and the desired body may in turn be seen as an erotic feast, in poem 48, as honey and wheat:

> Juventius, if I could play at kissing
> your honeyed eyes as often as I wished to,
> three hundred thousand games would not exhaust me;
> never could I be satisfied or sated,
> although the total of our osculations
> were greater than the ears of grain at harvest.   [1–6]

"If I were permitted," but of course he is not, and that resistance creates the drama. Juventius is an immovable feast, and when in poem 99 Catullus attempts to kiss something other than his lover's eyes, he is painfully rebuffed:

> While you were teasing me, honeyed Juventius, I
>   captured
>   a tiny kiss, sweeter than the sweetest ambrosia.
> I didn't make off with it, though—and haven't forgotten
>   how you kept me on the cross for over an hour!
>
>   [1–4]

Once again the beloved is an edible delicacy—*mellite Iuventi*, honeyed Juventius—whose kisses are even sweeter than ambrosia, the beverage of the gods. Had Catullus succeeded in his theft, his reward would have been the immortality conveyed by ambrosia, but as he did not, he receives the usual punishment for thieves: crucifixion. During the hour spent in Juventius' bad graces, he had to observe the real or pretended horror with which his lover dramatically purges his mouth. The explicit imagery Catullus uses to describe the operation suggests that he may also be not too far from revulsion at the thought of sexual intimacy:

> Soon as I did it, you fiercely commenced prophylaxis,
>   washing your lips and rubbing them dry with your
>   fingers

> to cleanse the infection of *me* from your dear mouth
>   completely,
>   as though you'd been soulkissed by some virulent
>   hooker!   [8–11]

The innocent kiss that tasted of immortality to the poet is now revealed as a life-threatening source of contagion to the resistant beloved: we return to that world of furtive sex in alleyways. The experience is so shocking to Catullus that the lingering taste of Juventius' kiss on his own mouth is turned into an aftertaste of the poison of the bitter and deadly hellebore plant. Catullus ends the poem with a playful promise that, from now on, he will steal no more kisses.

But the drama expands to include more characters, for Juventius has other admirers who, it would seem, are not as abstemious as Catullus. In poem 15 Catullus asks a modest favor of one of them, Aurelius:

> My soul is yours, in trust with my beloved,
> Aurelius. I ask a modest favor:
> if you have ever in your heart been anxious
> to keep a lover faithful and unworldly,
> see that my darling doesn't get in trouble.
> I'm not afraid of strangers getting at him,
> men in the streets preoccupied with business,
> rushing about too madly for seductions:
> it's *you* I really fear, you and your penis,
> which means no good to boys both nice and naughty!
>   [1–10]

One may doubt the seriousness of this poem and at the same time admit that the favor Catullus asks of Aurelius seems genuine: to preserve the innocence of Juventius from the hunger of Aurelius' penis. And the punishment with which Catullus threatens Aurelius for violation of his trust explicitly links sex and food; parts of a meal that should go in at one end will be stuffed in at the other:

But if infatuation's raging madness
urges you on to any monkey business,
ah! how I dread the end you'll come to, tortured
like an adulterer before the people:
feet bound together, nether door propped open
with a ripe bunch of radishes and mullets!   [14–19]

For Catullus, sexual hyperactivity is characterized as ravenous hunger: we have already seen Rufa having her dinner in the graveyard and Flavius, whose constant attentions to his secret mistress show in the excessive leanness of his flanks. And in poem 21, Aurelius is addressed, curiously, as *pater esuritionem*, father of starvations,

not just of these afflicting us at present,
but those as well of past and future ages   [2–3]

Catullus worries that Aurelius will teach this hunger and thirst to Juventius:

I wouldn't say a word, were you a fat man,
but how can I endure my boy enduring
lessons in drought and famine from the Master? [9–11]

For Catullus, the lean and hungry look is the sign of the lecher, not the political conspirator. Aurelius' desire is to the innocent sexuality of Juventius as theft is to the gift. The ravenous Aurelius will steal the vitality of Juventius and leave nothing in its place but sexual hunger.

And there is not only Aurelius, but Furius as well, against whom Catullus cautions Juventius in poem 24,

I'd sooner have you give the wealth of Midas
to one who has no servant and no money
than have you give yourself to his embraces.
"Why not?" you ask me. "Isn't he darling?"

                                                            Yes,

but Darling has no servant and no money.
Throw out my words, discount them if you want to,
but still he has no servant and no money.   [4–10]

Most probably the point of this is not to display Juventius as
an inattentive little gold digger but to caution him against an
unseemly connection with someone far below him in social
rank. It is difficult to know how seriously one should take all
this, given the absence of the fierce anger and pain with which
Catullus wrote about Lesbia. When he writes poem 23, a companion piece to the poem above, it turns into a small comic
masterpiece, a bizarre fantasia on the social, oral, and anal
consequences of poverty:

> You've got no servant, Furius, no money,
> no bedbug, no spider spinning by no fire—
> you've got a father, though, and a stepmother
> whose teeth can grind the toughest stone to gravel!
> It's beautiful, the life you lead with these two,
> your father and your father's withered woman.
> No wonder, for the three of you are thriving,
> your sound digestions undisturbed by worry:
> no fear of fires, of collapsing buildings,
> the knives of thieves, the venom of assassins,
> or any other routine urban perils.
> Your constitutions are as dry as horn is,
> or what (if anything) is even drier,
> thanks to your diet and your outdoor lifestyle.
> Remarkable, the way you go on living
> with neither sweat nor spittle—thus no hacking
> coughs, no runny noses. To these *nice* touches,
> add one last refinement: an asshole gleaming
> with all the radiance of polished silver!
> Ten times a year or less it opens, chucking
> a pellet harder than a bean or pebble—
> and each of them so nicely inoffensive,
> that if you crumble one between your fingers,
> it leaves no stain! O Furius, you prosper!
> Don't throw away all this, don't say it's nothing!
> You need a hundred thousand? No, stop asking:
> you have your fortune—but it can't be counted. [1–27]

Even though they are often hilariously and outrageously obscene, these poems reveal the outlines of a serious moral conflict. On the one hand there is rapacious greed, unbridled
orality, so set on devouring the world that it consumes at both
ends, indiscriminately stuffing the micturating mule-cunt mouth
of Aemilius and the *culus vorax* of Vibennius' lecherous son.
On the other hand, there are those restraining rules of social
behavior that commensality teaches us.

Inevitably the two must come into conflict, and often in
these poems the scene of their struggle is the convivium itself,
the place where morality reins in orality so that men may meet
in trusting negligence, off their guard with one another. It
would be difficult to exaggerate the importance of these periods of relaxed fellowship in a society where casual violence
was the norm. Stability depended on everyone following the
rules of the convivium; those rules were sometimes inflex-
ible—thou shalt not steal thy neighbor's napkin when he isn't
looking—and sometimes improvised for the nonce. At banquets, for instance, it was the custom for a man to be chosen
as *magister bibendi*, Lord of the Revels, whose job was to set the
proportions by which the company's wine would be cut with
water. In poem 27 Catullus gives us a drinking song from a
party where that office was performed (unusually and perhaps
even scandalously) by a woman whose feelings about the use
of water were in line with those of the poet:

> Waiter, Falernian! That fine old wine, boy:
> pour me another bowl and make it stronger.
> Postumia, the mistress of these revels,
> loaded as the vines are, she's laid the law down:
> go elsewhere, water. Go to where you're wanted,
> spoiler of wine, go—pass your sober days with
> sober people! Up Bacchus, undiluted.   [1–7]

Unlike the laws that hedge us all about, these rules were
designed to liberate, by promoting that playfulness from
which all art emerges. In the service of those rules is the poet
who celebrates them in poems like the one above and who also

enforces them by defining through his own behavior what is and is not elegant, what is and is not permissible.

And those who break the rules, whether out of malevolence or ignorance, are the natural targets of his satire.

In the poems written immediately before his journey to Bithynia, two subjects occupied Catullus' attentions: the failure of his relationship with Lesbia and the sudden, catastrophic death of his brother. After Bithynia, Lesbia is dismissed, to enter his subsequent poetry only as a target of abuse. But what of that promise he made in poem 65 to his brother:

> at certe semper amabo,
> semper maesta tua carmina morte canam

> but surely I will always love you,
> always your sad death will have its place in my singing
>   [11–12]

With the exception of poem 101, which must have been written during or shortly after the journey to Bithynia, there is no further reference to his brother's death. If we assume that Catullus' grief is genuine, then it seems curious that the subject does not find its way into the poems written after his homecoming. But we should not impose an awkwardly literal interpretation on poem 65 and assume that Catullus meant to spend the rest of his life in poetic sackcloth, telling sad tales of the death of his brother. Clearly, the poems of grief had already been written, and what he promises in these lines is what the poem in which they occur actually illustrates, a way of transforming lamentation into poetry, loss into art.

Poem 65 illustrates the way in which Catullus experienced the shock of a loved one's death, and the subsequent passages of lamentation, acceptance, and recovery. To the ancients, those stages in the lives of individuals seemed to have their parallels in the natural world, as the year turns from autumn's harvest, to winter's death, to the rebirth of life in the springtime. The principal myth associated with this cycle is that of

Persephone, the maiden seized by Hades to become his bride and the queen of the underworld. Persephone's father, Zeus, gave his approval to the seizure, but when her mother, Demeter, learned of it, she adamantly refused her consent. Zeus relented and sent the messenger Hermes to bring Persephone back, but because she had tasted a pomegranate given her by her lover, Hades, she was forced to spend a third of the year with him in the underworld, and the rest of the year with her mother on earth. For this reason the fleshy, blood-colored fruit of the pomegranate symbolized immortality to the Romans.

In the ending of poem 65, I think that we are meant to see a playful allusion to the myth of Persephone:

> just as the apple, a gift on the sly from her lover,
>   falls from the perfectly blameless lap of the virgin:
> oblivious wretch! she'd hidden it under her gown, but
>   rises politely, seeing her mama—and sends it
> hurtling out of its hiding place, bouncing and rolling
>   while a self-conscious scarlet flows over her sad face!

As in the myth, there is a triadic arrangement of figures: the mother, the lover, and the maiden, whose response to the revelation of the apple suggests that she is aware of herself as the object of contending interests between mother and lover. An apple is not a pomegranate, but for the Romans a pomegranate was a kind of apple, and our name for it derives from theirs: *pomum granatum*, the grained apple. Surely Catullus means us to see that apple—whether Persephone's or no—as a gift from the underworld, from death itself; for without the death of his brother and the poet's ensuing grief, that apple would never have appeared.

In a way poem 65 is a necessary prologue to all of these later poems, for its account of the poet's grief, his alienation from the Muses, and his recovery prepares us for the celebration of death transformed into life and life transformed into art. The period of his grief and alienation must have occurred before his journey to Bithynia in 57 B.C.: in the latter part of that journey and after his return to Italy, poetry once again had a place in his life, as the homecoming poems clearly show. We see all the elements of that recovery in place for the first time in poem 4, where the poet, safely delivered from death—both the physical dangers that threatened his own destruction and the pilgrimage to the site of his brother's grave—now acts as a host in the presence of his assembled guests. He offers to Castor and Pollux the gift that commemorates his deliverance, thanks to the services of his faithful craft, which now, like that poem in which it is enshrined, is offered up as an emblem of that deliverance, that transformation.

The restoration to life is at the same time a restoration to poetry and to the social body that poetry charms and eroticizes. And the promise made to his brother is kept also, for the poems that emerge from that experience have yet another charge, one described by Ezra Pound in his eighty-third canto:

> to carry our news
> εἰς χθονίους   to them that dwell under the earth
> begotten of air, that shall sing in the bower
> of Kore,[4]   Περσεφόνεια

III   VANISHING LINES

VII ON PASSIONATE VIRTUOSITY IN A POEM OF SOME LENGTH

> My feeling about technique in art is that it has about the same value as technique in love-making. That is to say, heartfelt ineptitude has its appeal and so does heartless skill; but what you want is passionate virtuosity.
> —John Barth

THE DARKNESS THAT CONCEALS THE MAKING OF CATULLUS' REPutation in his own time is never more irritating than in the case of poem 64: if only we knew what kind of public reception the poem received when it first appeared on the Roman scene! As one of those newfangled miniature epics that the neoterics were busily plumping at the expense of the traditional kind, poem 64 would have been fashionably novel; besides, the passions of mythological figures were popular subjects in Roman decorative arts, and Catullus' cinematic treatment of the loves of Peleus and Thetis, and of Theseus and Ariadne, may have made his poem accessible to a larger audience than the neoterics usually found. Nor could it have hurt that the poem was rather beautifully written, full of lines in which the elaborately artificial distribution of nouns and adjectives clamored self-consciously for admiration, and full of sharply etched scenes that provided a continual feast of good things for the mind's eye. No matter how its first public responded to it, this was clearly a masterpiece in the original sense: a work that demonstrated a young artist's ambition and accomplishment, an effort to establish him as a significant figure in the eyes of his contemporaries.

At one time there were other poems like it: Cinna's

Zmyrna, which Catullus praises in poem 95; the *Io* of Calvus; and the unfinished poem about Cybele by the otherwise un-known Caecilius of poem 35. All are now lost, with poem 64 the sole survivor of this once thriving genre. Our age, having no poems like it, has had little idea of what, if anything, to make of poem 64. This is not surprising: our ability to criticize a literary work depends ordinarily on our recognizing it in the context of similar entities, about which there exists a tradition of commentary to which we may refer in evaluating the work in question. We can criticize *Oedipus the King* because we have other Greek tragedies with which to compare it, as well as commentaries on it that extend from our time to Aristotle's; if we had only the play itself, we might find ourselves agreeing with Max Beerbohm: "A tense and peculiar family, the Oedi-puses."[1]

Today, nobody even knows what Catullus and his crowd called this kind of poem, but since the nineteenth century it has been known as an *epyllion*, a little epic. The term is useful in suggesting that the form was a deliberate, radical concen-tration of the traditional epic, but perhaps it is misleading as well, since its association with epic raises expectations that this particular epyllion is unable to satisfy. If we look in it for what we look for in epic—a fable of central importance to our cul-ture, the actions and passions of heroic or moral role models, or just a good, long read—poem 64 will be a disappointment.

It is, after all, only about the length of *The Waste Land*. On its surface, poem 64 appears to be little more than a sequence of mythological scenes set in the legendary Golden Age, mov-ing pictures that segue effortlessly into one another, governed, ever so mildly, by chronological order. Hero meets goddess, hero marries goddess; much of the rest of the poem is a de-scription of scenes embroidered on a coverlet spread over a couch in the hero's palace. Ariadne awakens to find herself abandoned by her lover Theseus and laments his betrayal; she beseeches Jove for vengeance, and as a result the hero's father, Aegeus, casts himself into the sea in despair, mistakenly be-lieving that his son is dead; the god Iacchus (a.k.a. Bacchus) is seen beating the bushes for Ariadne, whom he loves. We return from the coverlet to a description of the wedding feast of Peleus and Thetis, and then the poem concludes with the poet describing and condemning the sordid realities of everyday life.

Such a summary gives little indication of the real pleasures to be found in the poem: its unflagging energy, high passions, and continual movement; the elegant pathos of Ariadne's lament, the rich sensuality of the poem's imagery; the pleasure that the poet so clearly gives and takes in description. Nevertheless, a summary indicates how far removed we are from a conventional epic: no real conflict, little action, and most important, no vivid characters. Aeneas may be as wooden as some of Virgil's modern critics say he is, but Catullus makes no attempt whatsoever to bring Peleus and Thetis to life; only Ariadne in her lament, and Aegeus in his, manage to project themselves slightly beyond the gorgeous tapestry of the poem's descriptive impulse.

How then are we to read this poem? Is it simply a failed epic, a dead end? We know that Catullus and his friends were not out to replicate what had already been done in the epic. But what was their purpose? It is helpful to recall their situation as the modernists of their time: like twentieth-century modernists, the neoteric poets were in revolt against a tradition they considered outworn, against expectations they regarded as stifling. Their aim was to create an art that "no longer refer[red] back to an authority or tradition as its origin or goal, but aim[ed] at novelty, originality, and invention."[2] I quote the contemporary Italian novelist Italo Calvino on the writers of his own generation, since it seems to me that the relation of the neoteric epyllion to the traditional epic was analogous to the relation in our time of metafiction to the traditional novel. Such contemporary practitioners of metafiction as John Barth and Calvino offer us instances of a highly self-conscious art, aware of its freedom from the obligations of the past, and turning (as the neoterics did before them) to new subjects and to new ways of representing those subjects. Freedom from worn-out expectations leads not necessarily to license or chaos but more often to the discovery of new ways of conceiving forms and conventions, which, unlike the ones they replace, respond more directly to the intentions of the artist.

New ideas about structure lead to new ideas about representation—which lead to new ideas about structure. At any rate, evidence of new ideas about both poetic structure and the representation of imagery abounds in poem 64. What goes on in the poem is more like what goes on in Barth or Calvino than like what goes on in the *Iliad* or the *Odyssey.* We can't judge poem 64 by the criteria we would use for either the traditional novel or the Homeric epic. For example, critics who complained about the absence of unity in the poem's division between the events of the marriage feast and the events depicted on the coverlet are correct, but rather than carelessly neglecting epic unity, Catullus is providing us with the multiplicity of viewpoints we now recognize as polyphonic. Likewise deliberate is the poet's downplaying of traditional narrative, of character successively revealed through action. Narrative is replaced by subjective representation revealed in the poem's structure. "The unity of a book need not stem from its plot, but can be provided by its theme," Milan Kundera reminds us.[3] The unity of poem 64 derives from its theme, and its theme is its structure; that is, the shape of the poem is itself thematic, which means that, whatever else the poem is about, it is about itself as a work of art.

The strategies of representation Catullus employs in poem 64 were in all likelihood influenced by developments occurring in the work of the visual artists of his time. This is not surprising: in our age, modernism broke out in poetry, music, and painting at almost the same time; the concerns of modernism were seen as translatable from one art form to another. Wallace Stevens writes, "To a large extent, the problems of poets are the problems of painters."[4] Painting ventured into abstraction before poetry did, and often what was most experimental in modern poetry came from the attempt to respond to technical advances first made on canvas: the *Cantos* of Ezra Pound and Gertrude Stein's *Tender Buttons* follow Picasso and Braque; William Carlos Williams' *Spring And All* is likewise obligated to his friendship with the early modernist American artists.

While the neoterics were busy transforming Roman poetry, Roman art was being similarly changed by the anonymous artists whose frescoes adorned the walls of Roman houses. From about 60 B.C., the artists of the so-called second, or architectural, style moved beyond painting polychrome panels into figuration. The houses that these artists worked on were long and narrow, extending back perpendicularly from the street on horizontal axes. The long interior lateral walls gave ample space for decoration, which at first consisted of the representation of imaginary architectural forms *beyond* the wall, as though the artist's first concern were his wish to transcend the constraints imposed by the wall itself. Figures followed forms: mythological scenes, episodes from Homer. Having abolished the wall, Roman artists invited gods, goddesses, and heroes into the homes of their patrons, mingling mortals and immortals in the same way Catullus does in poem 64.

Of greatest interest to us for reading Catullus' poem, however, is the Roman artists' fascination with creating the illusion of depth in their paintings. This they did in two ways. In any scene, one figure could be represented as deeper than another if it were smaller and placed higher on the picture plane:

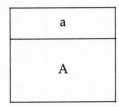

But Roman artists were also capable of a more sophisticated form of perspective, in which lines of perspective converged on a vertical axis (or axes) at or near the center of the painting:

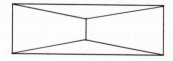

This vanishing line perspective gives a realistic illusion of depth to their work.

The sudden opening up of space, the breaking down of the wall that separated this world from the mysterious one beyond it, must have been liberating to the artistic imagination. But how could that freedom be translated into poetry? How could words be arranged in lines and then in scenes that would give the illusion of depth?

Let us begin with an observation about the length of poem 64. Modern editors don't count the half line after line 23 or the line missing after line 253 and therefore describe the poem as 408 lines long. Well, that is its current length, but Catullus originally wrote a poem of 410 lines, one and a half of which have been lost in transmission. The point is not insignificant: the number of lines in poem 64 matters in the same way (and for the same reasons) as the number of cantos in Dante's *Commedia*. The fact that the missing lines have been ignored has obscured from the poet's readers the extraordinary symmetry of his poem.

Catullus arranged the 410 lines in eight compartments, each of which is composed of one or more scenes. These compartments are of no fixed length: the longest consists of eighty-five lines, the shortest, fourteen. The compartments themselves have been composed so that the first four comprise almost the entire first half of the poem, lines 1–202, and the last four comprise almost all of the second half of the poem, lines 208–410. Between these two sections lies a brief bridge, a single sentence of five lines. In the third of these five lines (which is of course the last line of the first half of the poem) something happens: Jove nods his assent to Ariadne's prayer for vengeance, providing the link between the two halves of the poem.

Poem 64 can be read as a continuous narrative in chronological order, with one event being succeeded by another from beginning to end. However, as I mentioned in chapter II, the compartments of the poem have been arranged so that they relate to one another according to the rhetorical figure called chiasmus. That is to say, the two outermost compartments, the first and the eighth, are the unequally divided halves of a temporal and thematic continuity, as are the second and the seventh, the third and the sixth, and the fourth and the fifth. The structure of the compartments may be represented by the following diagram:

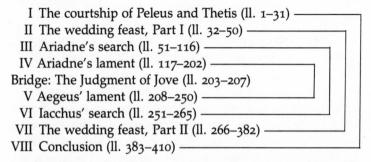

I The courtship of Peleus and Thetis (ll. 1–31)

II The wedding feast, Part I (ll. 32–50)

III Ariadne's search (ll. 51–116)

IV Ariadne's lament (ll. 117–202)

Bridge: The Judgment of Jove (ll. 203–207)

V Aegeus' lament (ll. 208–250)

VI Iacchus' search (ll. 251–265)

VII The wedding feast, Part II (ll. 266–382)

VIII Conclusion (ll. 383–410)

The first and eighth compartments span the greatest periods of time in the poem: the first deals entirely with the legendary Golden Age, when gods and mortals intermingled; the eighth begins with a description of these activities and concludes with a description of contemporary degeneracy. The second and seventh compartments span a far more circumscribed period: the morning and evening of the day of the wedding feast.

The temporal relations among the four inner compartments, whose scenes are depicted on the coverlet, are somewhat more complicated than those of the outer compartments, because the coverlet is a work of art and as such is timeless, existing in the same order of being as the shield of Achilles. Yet the inner compartments are also continuous with one another and with the four outer compartments of the poem in both chronological and chiastic order.

The third and sixth compartments continue the twofold process of lessening the amount of time suspended in each compartment and of narrowing down the amount of time between compartments. In the sixth compartment, Iacchus' search for Ariadne occurs on the same day as (and very shortly after) Ariadne awakens to find Theseus gone. Once again, the third and sixth compartments are narrative and thematic halves: the mortal Theseus betrays Ariadne's unsanctified passion; that betrayal will be balanced and completed by the licit love of the immortal Iacchus, who is seen in the sixth compartment searching for Ariadne, the absent object of his affections, just as in the third compartment Ariadne searches for Theseus, the vanished object of her passions.

The fourth and fifth compartments, two halves of another whole, bring the compression of time to its inevitable end.

Read chronologically, the first and eighth compartments are our entrance and exit, the beginning and end of the poem. Read chiastically, the two compartments are the separated halves of a whole, offering us two different views of the relationship between the gods and mortals: the Golden Age, when the two orders mingled and even fell in love with one another, and our own degenerate times, when, appalled by human misbehavior, the gods have withdrawn from our presence.

In the first compartment, Catullus gives us a glorious description of the pleasures of that happiest time of all ages:

> They say it was pine sprung from the crown of Mount Pelion
> which swam clear across the perilous waters of Neptune
> to the river Phasis in the realm of King Aeetes,
> back in those days when the best men the Argives could muster,
> eager to carry the golden fleece out of Colchis,
> dared to go racing their swift ship over the ocean
> and stirred its cerulean surface with oars made of firwood.

> Athena, who keeps the towers protecting the city,
> she fashioned this hurtling carriage for those young
>   men,
> she joined the timbers of pine to the curve of the firm
>   keel.
> That ship, the Argo, first taught the seas about sailing.
> And so, when its sharp beak plowed down through the
>   wind-driven waters,
> when it churned the billows white by the work of its
>   oarblades,
> incredulous sea nymphs came bobbing right up to the
>   surface,
> eager to catch just a glimpse of this unheard-of marvel!
> If ever sailors were witness to wonders, those men
>   were,
> who saw with their very own eyes the Nereids rising,
> barebreasted mermaids afloat on the whiteheaded
>   ocean.
> They say it was then that Peleus burned to have Thetis,
> who raised no objections to taking a mortal husband,
> and the Father himself judged that they ought to be
>   married.   [1–21]

From the first line of the poem, Catullus composes the scene to give us the illusion of spatial and temporal depth: we begin with a headlong rush from precipice to plain, background to foreground, past to present. The earliest action of the poem is firmly located in the legendary past: "They say it was pine," and placed a distant height, "sprung from the crown of Mount Pelion." Immediately we plunge to sea level with the Argonauts, aided in the construction of their vessel by Athena, in the poem's first felicitous instance of mortal-immortal intermingling.

On the flat plane of the ocean, we move into the present as we observe the Argo churning up a wake. In this sharply detailed foreground, sea nymphs rush to the surface to behold the daring mortals, and the mortals enjoy the sight of the barebreasted sea nymphs—as we do, placed directly in front of the scene, as viewers of a fresco. Catullus has composed the scene as a triangle whose apex (Pelion) comprises both the past and the background of the scene, and whose bases (Peleus and Thetis) are foregrounded in the scene's present moment:

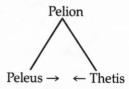

The eye is the organ of desire: no sooner does the exchange occur, when "they say it was then that Peleus burned to have Thetis."

In this poem the consequences of sight, whether delight or despair, are immediate, and so the wedding scenes follow in the poem's second compartment. Again, the second and seventh compartments form two contrasting halves of a chronological and thematic whole, describing the two parts of the wedding feast; in the second compartment, the mortal wedding guests arrive at the palace of Peleus, and in the seventh compartment, they scatter and the immortal guests arrive.

Consisting of a pair of brief, closely related scenes, the second compartment is also composed with a painterly eye. Both scenes emphasize convergence: in the first scene, the Thessalian wedding guests, temporarily suspending their agricultural pursuits, converge on the palace:

> And so at last, on the appointed day of the wedding,
> the people of Thessaly throng to his palace together
> in celebration, filling its chambers completely,
> gifts in their hands, expressions of joy on their faces.
> Cieros is emptied, they pour from Pthiotic Tempe,
> from the houses of Crannon and out through the gates
>   of Larissa
> they come to Pharsalus and gather under its rooftops.
> The land's left untilled, the backs of the oxen grow
>   tender,

the curved rake no longer loosens the soil of the
    vineyard,
the young bull no longer breaks up the packed earth
    with the plowshare,
the dresser of vines no longer cuts back the branches of
    shade trees,
and a thin film of rust spreads over the idle equipment.
                                                        [32–43]

The second scene draws our eye directly into the hero's palace,
through a narrowing of successive rooms. Our appreciation of
the composition of this scene depends on our recreating in our
mind's eye the alternating light and dark of successive rooms,
converging as one looks down along the horizontal axis of a
Roman house until we see the first of the poem's vanishing
lines:

But in his opulent palace, great chambers receding
create a vista resplendent with glittering gold and silver;
ivory glows on the couch legs, the cups on the table gleam,
and all of that house is gay with the splendor of riches.
A couch fit for the goddess is set in the center,
one made of polished Indian ivory draped with a purple
coverlet steeped in the crimson dye of the sea conch.
                                                        [44–50]

The scene continues without a pause to the next compartment,
and our first sight of Ariadne:

For there, staring out from the resonant seacoast of Dia,
Ariadne watches the swift fleet of Theseus leaving,
and in her heart an unrestrainable fury arises,
for she still can't believe that she sees what she is
    seeing!
—no wonder, for sleep had deceived her: just now
    awakened,
she finds herself coolly abandoned there on the
    seashore.

Ungrateful, her lover flees, striking the waves with his
 oarblades,
leaving the storm winds to make good on his broken
 promise.
The weeping daughter of Minos stands still in the
 seaweed,
stands watching him in the distance: a Maenad in
 marble,
rocked by the waves of her anguish, she stands there
 and watches;
her golden hair is no longer tied up in its headband,
the delicate veil no longer covers her torso,
her tender white breasts are no longer bound up in their
 halter;
all of her garments have slipped to her feet in
 confusion,
adrift in the salt tide that evenly scoured the coastline.

[53–63]

The first three compartments all situate the reader as viewer,
placed directly in front of the scenes depicted in the poem.
Roman artists tended to place their figures on the axis of the
painting, facing the spectator, as Catullus does to great dramatic effect here in the third compartment, with this stunning
vision of a half-naked woman standing in the sea foam, her
disordered garments and bare breasts exciting pity and pru-
rience in equal measure. The scene owes its erotic tension to
the way in which Catullus has stationed us as spectators-
voyeurs-readers in the place of Theseus: our view of Ariadne
is the hero's view as his ships sail away from the island. And
because we are free neither to go to her nor to turn away from
her, the poet takes advantage of us, forces his readers to identify with her in her frozen moment of abandonment.

Earlier motifs are subtly repeated or altered: Ariadne's
bare breasts remind us of the similarly unhaltered Naiads in
the first compartment; love at first sight *then* is balanced by
despair at last glimpse *now*. Individual scenes are presented as

a whole, not narrated sequentially; as a result, they are spatially deep but temporally flat. And so, when Catullus wishes to explain Ariadne's situation, he must resort to a flashback in which we see the origin of her passions for the hero, how "When she first caught sight of that handsome stranger, / Ariadne kept her eyes fixed on him until they took fire." Once again, sight leads to instantaneous and overwhelming passion, causing her to betray her half-brother the Minotaur, whose battle with Theseus is described in an extended metaphor that repeats an earlier motif:

> Think of an oak or a conebearing pine tree that oozes
> with rosin, shaking its branches high up on Mount
>   Taurus;
> one which a fierce storm, wrenching the grain of its
>   timber
> uproots and sends hurtling off to spread terrible havoc
> for a great distance, until it lies prone in destruction:
> then think of Theseus over the overcome monster
> vainly tossing its horns in the unresisting breezes.
>
> [106–112]

The oak or pine on Mount Taurus reminds us of the pine on Mount Pelion with which the poem begins. We note also a repetition of the movement from height to base: in the foreground, on the picture plane, two figures are engaged in a fierce struggle. The downward motion creates illusory depth, the equivalent of perspective in painting.

The center of the poem, the vertical axis on which all sight lines converge, is the mast of Theseus' ship as it disappears over the horizon.

On either side of that line are the fourth and fifth compartments of the poem, governed by simultaneity and synchronicity; not only do the events they describe occur at the same time, but the two compartments display numerous thematic coincidences. In both compartments, the carelessness of Theseus brings misery to the two people who love him most,

Ariadne and Aegeus, both of whom search the horizon for what turns out to be (with tragic irony in the case of Aegeus) their last glimpse of the hero.

Both compartments are composed in much the same way: a few lines set the scene, followed by a dramatic monologue in which the protagonist rehearses her or his grief. Lesser details likewise echo one another: Ariadne rushes down from the mountain to the seaside at the beginning of the fourth compartment; at the end of the fifth, Aegeus flings himself from the height of the Acropolis into the sea.

The period of time contained in the two compartments continues to diminish: the fourth and fifth compartments occur in little more than the time it takes each protagonist to recite her or his lament. Most important, however, is the fact that the events depicted in the fourth and fifth compartments occur simultaneously. Ariadne stares off at the horizon in search of her lover: "By now," she says, "he must be half-done with his journey." At this point, it is not clear if she can still see him, though the logic of the poem (as well as the vanishing line that links the two innermost compartments) requires Ariadne to last glimpse Theseus' ship as its mast disappears over the horizon, precisely the moment when the ship appears to Aegeus. And so it happens:

> So, when the hero entered his home, it was darkened
> by mourning, and he received for himself as much sorrow
> as he had thoughtlessly given the daughter of Minos,
> *who kept a sad watch as his ship sank into the distance,*
> *dwelling on all of those cares with which she'd been wounded.*
>   [246–250]

When two events occur simultaneously, the time between them has been compressed as tightly as possible. Between the two innermost compartments, there is room only for an event that lies altogether outside of time, when immortal Jove gives his assent to Ariadne's prayer for vengeance. This happens in the five-line bridge between the two halves of the poem. The pivotal moment brings the first half of the poem to a close:

When she had emptied her heart of all of its sorrows,
anxiously seeking revenge for the way she'd been treated,
the ruler of heaven assented, majestically nodding,
and with that gesture the earth and the rough seas were
    shaken,
and the stars leapt in the firmament, quivering brightly.

[203–207]

Catullus certainly intended this two-part division, and so
we might reasonably ask whether there is any difference between the two halves of the poem. The first four compartments
are subtly but unmistakably characterized by images of creation and convergence, whereas the last four are just as certainly characterized by images of destruction and dispersal.
The energies of the first half of the poem converge on the vanishing line of Theseus' mast, and those of the second half scatter from it, in the way the lines of sight in a Roman painting
intersect the vanishing line:

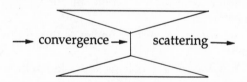

And so, in the first compartment, we see Peleus and Thetis coming together out of disparate realms to fall in love, creating new order in marriage; likewise, we see the goddess
Athena creating the vessel that carries Peleus to Thetis. The
second compartment contains two literal images of convergence: the Thessalians' arrival at the hero's palace and the convergence of all eyes upon the coverlet itself. The betrayal of
Ariadne by Theseus (as well as her betrayal of the Minotaur)
introduces disorder into the third compartment, but Catullus
spends fewer lines describing the plight of Ariadne abandoned
than he does recounting the flashback dealing with Theseus'
arrival at Knossos and the way in which the lovers' particular
convergence began.

The second half of the poem is dominated by images of dispersal and destruction, beginning with the death of Aegeus. It is worth noting that Catullus does not tell the story of Aegeus in chronological order: to do so, he would have had to begin with an image of divergence, the hero Theseus' departure from Athens and his father's loving lament for his son. Conversely, in the sixth compartment, Iacchus' search for Ariadne—an image of future convergence not to be realized in the poem—is overwhelmed by the poet's vivid description of the disorderly acts of the Maenads:

> But in another scene, flourishing Iacchus swaggered,
> surrounded by drunken Sileni and wanton young Satyrs;
> burning with love, he was searching for you, Ariadne.
>
> . . . .
>
> and Maenads also, who raged all around in a rapture,
> crying "Euhoe! Euhoe!" as their heads crazily nodded.
> Some of them whirled their weapons, spears tipped
>   with vineleaves;
> some tossed about the limbs of a bull they'd
>   dismembered,
> and some were girding their bodies with writhing
>   serpents
> or worshipping ritual emblems kept hidden in baskets,
> emblems which only initiates ever uncover.
> Others with uplifted hands were beating their tambours
> or shrilly clashing their hollow bronze cymbals together;
> many of them had horns which were raucously blaring,
> and the barbaric flute whirled out its hideous noises.
>
> [251–265]

Certainly there is a literal image of destruction and dispersal in the dismembered bull, whose death necessarily reminds us of the Minotaur's in the second compartment, a death seen in an elaborate simile rather than in realistic detail.

The seventh compartment, which describes the second half of the wedding feast, is the most varied and complex in

its treatment of images of convergence and dispersal. The compartment opens on a scene of dispersal, as the mortal wedding
guests, sated in their desire to see the coverlet, take their leave:

> you've seen the west wind rile the calm sea in the
>   morning,
> how it herds the steepening wavelets, herds them
>   before it
> as Dawn ascends to the gates of the journeying Sun;
> those waves move slowly at first, urged on by a mild
>   wind,
> and advance with a muted sound of continuous
>   laughter;
> but after the wind has arisen, they run on together
> and from a great distance they gleam with reflections of
>   crimson:
> so, moving out of the palace and out of its courtyard,
> the mortal wedding guests drifted off in every direction.
>   [270–278]

At once the immortal wedding guests arrive, beginning with
Chiron the centaur, who (like the pine trees of line 1) descends
from the summit of Pelion to join the guests converging on the
palace.

When the immortals are settled into their places, the
Three Fates begin their song for the wedding feast, a song
whose theme is convergence and dispersal. Convergence is expressed throughout the song in the refrain that ends each
stanza: *Run, spindles, run, drawing the threads that wait for the
weaving*. A pattern emerges when disparate lives, like separate
strands, converge and are woven together.

After a stanza of conventional praise for the distinguished
lineage of Peleus, the first image of convergence shows the
bride and groom together on their wedding night:

> Hesperus will be here soon with those gifts which the
>   newly
> married all long for; the bride will follow him closely,

flooding your heart with love that will charm you
    completely
as she lies by you at night in the tenderest slumber,
asleep with her delicate arms clasping your strong neck.
    Run, spindles, run, drawing the threads that wait for
      the weaving.

No house before this has sheltered such a great passion,
no love has ever linked lovers in any such union
as this one which joins Peleus and Thetis together
                          [329–337]

Immediately, however, the song of the Parcae, as the Fates are
also known, changes as they sing of the mortal offspring of
that union: the blessed convergence of the two lovers creates
Achilles, a hero who seems to personify the force that tears
down and disperses. Of the song's thirteen stanzas, seven describe Achilles' destructive propensities, rising steadily to a
horrific climax when the hero, unsated by a lifetime of slaughter, demands an especially cruel sacrifice from beyond the
grave:

                      the gift given his spirit
in death, when the hero's high-heaped, circular
    mounded barrow
is graced with the snowy limbs of the sacrificed virgin

  . . . .

that lofty tomb will be drenched with the blood of
    Polyxena,
struck down like a beast under the double-edged
    axeblade,
knees buckling as she pitches her headless corpse
    forward.   [363–365, 369–371]

What are we to make of the maiden's head at the wedding
feast? I don't believe that the strangeness of this moment in
the poem can be easily exaggerated: the carnage of warfare and
the horror of human sacrifice are not themes that lend themselves easily to a marriage song. Directly after the horrendous

spectacle, the Parcae return to a more appropriate conclusion
for a song at a wedding feast:

> Get going then, join those passions your hearts have
> desired;
> now let the bridegroom take the goddess in fortunate
> union,
> and let the bride be given right now to her eager new
> husband.
> Run, spindles, run, drawing the threads that wait for
> the weaving.
>
> The nurse who returns to attend her early tomorrow
> will find that her neck can't be circled by yesterday's
> ribbon:
> Run, spindles, run, drawing the threads that wait for
> the weaving   [373–379]

This startling conjunction of images of savage violence
and tender passion has not received the attention it deserves.
The song of the Parcae continues the rhythm established at the
beginning of the seventh compartment: an image of dispersal
as the mortal wedding guests scatter is succeeded by an image
of convergence as the immortal guests descend on the marriage feast. The Parcae sing first of the erotic convergence of
Peleus and Thetis, then of the destructive powers of Achilles,
and then of Peleus and Thetis once again. Necks figure prominently in all three passages, illustrating harmony, horror, and
erotic fulfillment. In the first, Thetis is depicted as blissfully
sleeping alongside her new husband, with her arms encircling
his neck; in the second, Polyxena's headless corpse pitches forward, drenching the tomb of Achilles with the blood pouring
from her neck; in the last, Catullus says that the serving maid
who attends Thetis on the morning after the wedding will discover, as proof that she has lost her virginity, that her neck
cannot be encircled by the same ribbon that she wore when
she was a maiden.

And what of Polyxena? Her appearance at the wedding

feast serves several functions. From the middle of the poem
onward, Catullus has been emphasizing violence and dispersal: the sacrifice of Polyxena represents the climax of increased
disorder. Polyxena and Achilles also form a pair of lovers to
contrast with Peleus and Thetis in the second half of the poem,
just as Theseus and Ariadne contrast with them in the first
half. In order to create life, Peleus will shed the hymeneal
blood of Thetis on their wedding night; in an ironic parody of
that act, the life they bring forth, Achilles, sheds the blood of
Polyxena, taking the maiden's head rather than her maiden-
head. Polyxena marries the personification of the powers of
destruction; the blood of the maiden drenches the tomb of the
hero, enlarging those powers. Convergence, dispersal, convergence: the process is cyclical, endless, inescapable. The love
of Peleus and Thetis will produce the death-dealing Achilles,
but the lovers cannot avoid their fate: they accept it as a part
of life.

The poem concludes in the eighth compartment with a
contrast between the Golden Age and Catullus' own morally
sordid era; but even where the poet is describing the earlier
time, the images are weighted on the side of violence, sacrifice,
and warfare, rather than the erotic bliss of the first compartment:

> Often Jove the Father, paying a regular visit
> to one of his temples during the annual feast days
> would see a hundred bulls crash to earth in his honor.
> And Liber would rove on the peak of Parnassus, driving
> his Maenads, who shook their wild hair and cried out,
>   "Euhoe!"
> Then all of Delphi came pouring out of the city
> to greet the young god with smoke wreathing their altars.
> And often in deathbearing warfare, Mars or Athena
> the mistress of Triton, or Nemesis, Virgin of Rhamnus,
> would show themselves to encourage bands of armed
>   men   [388–397]

Poem 64 is, finally, an inexplicable mystery. If we read the poem without any awareness of the symbolic structure that underlies it, our attention moves easily from scene to scene, compartment to compartment; we are almost unaware of any intervening barriers. Transitions are casual, if not illusory. But once we become aware of the structure, the shimmering surface breaks up, and the elaborate architectonics of the poem draw us into a sophisticated meditation on the nature of time and the representation of space.

The poem's structure creates and decorates a symbolic house. But to what end? We are given eight compartments, each composed of scenes organized visually to create the illusion of depth, each set on a horizontal axis: on that line we follow the hero Theseus until he vanishes. The most striking thing about Theseus is his absence from the poem: he is the hero as absence, a void at the center of the poem, as mysteriously distant from his story as Bartleby, as motiveless in his cruelty as Iago. Gone when Ariadne awakens, it is as though he exists only to prove the futility of human actions, to show us that it is mortal fate to desire helplessly, like Ariadne, like Aegeus, like Iacchus, all equally helpless in rage, in grief, and in love.

Despite the futility of human actions, in the face of a universe constantly moving toward increasing disorder, the artist builds his house. Its symbolic structure is a way of reversing or at least holding back the disorder of the universe, a temporary stay against the forces it describes. Not incidentally, the occasion of the poem is a marriage feast, when two lovers unite in a moment that goes on beyond and even without them, a moment which cannot be controlled, but must, as here, be celebrated by gods and by mortals.

VIII LIFTING THE POET'S FINGERPRINTS: A READING OF POEMS 61–68

OUR FINAL TASK IN READING POEM 64 IS TO SEE IT IN ITS CONTEXT as an integral and interactive part of the sequence composed of poems 61 to 68. I use the term *sequence* deliberately here, for this is not simply an unconnected series of long poems, passively occupying space according to the convenience of a copyist. Rather, these poems constitute a single poem in eight parts, each of which may be read as a poem by itself, and each having its place in the sequence as a function of its relations with the other poems in the sequence.

That assertion is likely to be met with a good deal of skepticism: how can poems so various in their meters, genres, styles, and subjects possibly constitute a unified sequence? Poem 61 is an epithalamion, in the glyconic meter for the wedding of one Manlius Torquatus and his bride, Junia (or Vinia); poem 62 is a debate in hexameter between choruses of young men and young women at a marriage feast; it is succeeded by a narrative poem about the goddess Cybele's favorite, the unfortunate Attis, written in Cybele's favorite meter, the galliambic. Then comes poem 64, our epyllion, also in hexameter; these four poems in three different meters are followed by four poems in the same meter, the elegiac. The first, poem 65, is a verse epistle introducing poem 66, a translation of a poem by Callimachus. The translation is followed by a naughty, comic dialogue between the poet and a talking door in poem 67. Finally, there is poem 68, another verse epistle (or perhaps two verse epistles), written in two distinctly different styles, and addressed to someone who could be named Manius Allius, Allius Mallius, Manlius Torquatus, or almost any two of the above; this brief catalog does not exhaust the difficulties presented by poem 68. What kind of unity may we expect to find in poems as apparently disparate as these?

I think that the largest obstacle to seeing these eight poems as parts of a single poem is our long habit of reading them as separate works, each complete in itself and each significantly different from its neighbors. That's been a satisfactory habit, so why change it? The only reason is that Catullus seems to have had something different in mind. In order to find out what he intended, we first have to assume the possibility that these eight poems constitute a single poem; if that is the case, how would we be able to show it?

The grin on this particular Cheshire Cat is its structure, the system of relationships that bind the poems together, creating a subtle and complex unity; it is only that structure that keeps us (once we have seen it) from reading these as eight separate poems. Just as in poem 64, the structure is provided by the chiastic figure of inversion: the two outermost poems, the middle poems on either side, and the next two innermost poems are related to one another and to poem 64:

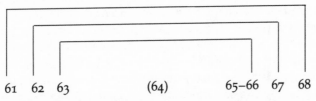

61 62 63 (64) 65–66 67 68

Each of the six poems surrounding poem 64 contrasts with its opposite number metrically and thematically; in order to preserve balance, the innermost pair reverses the direction of the thematic contrast.

The sequence is composed of poems that treat two different but closely related themes: love as sanctified in marriage
and love as unsanctified erotic passion. How do the parts of
this sequence interact with one another to express the theme?
Let us begin at the center of the sequence, with poem 64.

Like the other poems in the sequence, it is both a poem
in its own right as well as a knot through which the energies
of the sequence pass and are transformed. But it is the longest
poem in the sequence, and it differs from the others in two
important ways: the first is that it is not part of an interactive
pair; like the five-line bridge at its center, poem 64 stands by
itself. It is also the only poem in the sequence capable of exploring both themes, unsanctified passion (Theseus and Ariadne) and the erotic fulfillment possible in marriage (Peleus
and Thetis).

The other poems in the sequence explore one or the other
of these two themes—never both—and they are arranged on
either side of poem 64 to reflect that division of concerns. Thus,
poems 61 and 62 show passion sanctified by marriage, while
poem 63 shows unsanctified erotic obsession; as in a mirror on
the other side of poem 64, poems 65–66 show the sanctity of
marriage, while poems 67 and 68 deal with the unsanctified
passions of adulterous love.

Poem 64 was composed so that its outermost compartments present a contrast between the Golden Age, when gods
and mortals mingled, fell in love, and even married, and later
debased times, characterized by sexual betrayal and degeneracy. The poems on either side of poem 64 reflect that division
as well. Poems 61 through 63 are characterized by the intermingling of gods and mortals; in poem 61 the god Hymen is
summoned to join the wedding party; poem 62 takes place in
a fantasized Greek setting; poem 63 deals with the relationship
between a goddess and a mortal. On the other side of poem
64, poem 65 (a prelude to the translation in poem 66) deliberately states a contemporary, personal theme. Poem 67 deals
with the sordid realities of a contemporary marriage, and
poem 68 explores an episode of adultery in the poet's own life.

It is as though the energies concentrated in poem 64 were

allowed to radiate outward into the poems surrounding it. Each of these poems represents a part of poem 64 in terms of either the contrast between the Golden Age and contemporary decadence, sanctified and unsanctified passions, an idealistic view of human relationships possible in a time when gods and heroes mingled, or the unblinking realism necessary in our degenerate times.

At first glance, poems 63 and 65–66 might appear to have nothing in common beyond their author. Poem 63 is a vivid narrative of the destructive erotic obsession of the mortal Attis for the goddess Cybele, while poem 66 is a graceful present made to an Alexandrian queen, a fanciful account of how a lock of her hair became the constellation known as the *Coma Berenice*. But the two poems are a perfect example of the contrast between the themes of destructive erotic obsession and the erotic fulfillment possible in marriage. In poem 63, Attis is the humiliated love-slave of Cybele, the implacable *dominatrix*, while Berenice, in poem 66, is the devoted and faithful bride of her royal husband.

The two poems contrast with one another thematically and metrically, but there are also a number of subtle and intriguing similarities between them. The protagonists of both poems perform sacrifices to bring them closer to their beloveds: Attis castrates himself in order to become a more acceptable devotee of his Cybele, and Berenice cuts off a lock of her hair as a sacrifice to the gods for the safe return of her husband. There is, however, a striking difference between the results of their actions: Berenice's sacrifice rises up to heaven and is transformed into a glittering constellation, while Attis' offering bleeds into the dust of the earth.

Both Attis and Berenice experience a gender change: the emasculated Attis feels himself to be a woman and cries out in dismay,

> Must I now be called a priestess? Must I be Cybele's handmaid?
> A maenad—a broken part of what I was—a barren creature? [63, 68–69]

Catullus stresses Berenice's valor, however, a characteristic his
age would see as masculine:

> when the King (her husband for only a few brief hours)
>   went off to wage a vengeful war on the Syrians,
> [he] carried to battle the sweet traces of amorous combat,
>   spoils which a virgin had yieldingly defended.
>
> > [66, 11–14]

The amorous combatant falls into deep despond when her husband leaves; her severed lock of hair notices the queen's altered emotional state and comments on it:

> > I saw you devoured by sorrow,
> >   entirely preoccupied with your misfortune,
> > showing no sign of your spirit. But I who have known
> >   you
> >   ever since childhood, I've never doubted your
> >   courage!
> > Or have you forgotten that boldness by which your
> >   royal husband
> >   was won, when no one else dared to be bolder?
>
> > [23–28]

Both poems also contain references to Venus and the true or
pretended hatred she inspires. In poem 63, the devotees of
Cybele are set in real opposition to the goddess of love: Attis,
urging them on, addresses them as "you who've emasculated
yourselves out of hatred for Venus." Berenice's lock asks,

> Is Venus *hated* by brides? Is that superabundance
>   of tears which they shed outside the bridal chamber,
> are they false tears, shed just to dampen the joys of
>   their parents?
>   Of course they are, really: I swear it by heaven!
>
> > [15–18]

The hymeneal blood shed by young brides like Berenice has
its counterpart in the blood shed by Attis in his act of self-
mutilation.

One other similarity between poems 63 and 66 remains to be mentioned. Poem 66 is a translation of a Callimachean original, as Catullus explains in poem 65, the prelude that accompanies it. Many scholars have believed that poem 63 is also a translation or imitation: C. J. Fordyce writes, "Its spirit is so Greek that it seems certain that Catullus has translated or adapted a Greek original."[1] If that is indeed the case, the Greek origin of the poem would explain its pairing with the Alexandrian poem 66.

Poems 62 and 67, the next interactive pair in the sequence, playfully echo the contrasting subjects and meters of poems 63 and 66. Poem 62 is another marriage poem, this time a spirited debate between a chorus of young men and a chorus of young women on the rewards and satisfactions—or lack thereof—of marriage. Both sides present highly unrealistic positions, formed out of great expectations on the part of the young men, who sing of marriage with the enthusiasm of stockbrokers discussing a corporate merger, and high anxiety on the part of the young women, who see their potential mates as nothing less than the pillagers of cities:

The Young Women:
Hesperus, what fire fiercer than yours crosses heaven?
—you who can tear the young child from her mother's
    embraces,
tear the poor terrified child from the lap of her mother
and hand the chaste daughter over to an eager young
    man!
Do those who sack cities carry on any more fiercely?
Hymen O Hymenaee, Hymen, come now, O Hymenaee.

The Young Men:
Hesperus, what fire fairer than yours shines in heaven?
—you who confirm with your flame the agreement of
    marriage
arranged by the husband, arranged by the parents
    beforehand,

but left unfinished until your bright torch has arisen.
What gift from heaven surpasses this fortunate hour?
Hymen O Hymenaee, Hymen, come now, O Hymenaee.

[62, 20–31]

What the two choruses have in common is a highly unrealistic
set of expectations derived from fear and desire rather than
from experience.

Poem 67 hilariously counters the position of the inexpe-
rienced innocents with a generous helping of sordid realities.
The contrasts are thematic and metrical: poem 62 is in hexa-
meters, poem 67 in the elegiac meter; however, the forms are
parallel, since poem 67 is also a dialogue, between Catullus
and a door who describes the sexual mischief going on inside
his house. It is an explicit, realistic commentary on the idealized view of marriage seen in poem 62, where both the young
men and the young women assume that the bride is *always*
chaste:

Door:
Well, to begin with, the story she came here a
        virgin
    just isn't true, although her first mate never touched
        her:
his little dirk dangled—a limp beet is scarcely more
        languid—
    and never managed to make a dent in his tunic.
But his father, they say, ravished her in his son's own
        bed,
    bringing disgrace down on that miserable household
. . . .
Often I've overheard her, in furtive conversations
    discussing affairs alone with her servant women,
giving the names of the men I've just mentioned, as
        though she
    never imagined that I could hear her—or tattle.

[67, 19–28, 41–44]

Impotence, incest, and casual promiscuity: these represent the realities behind the social masks, the failures of the ideal to materialize, and the personal arrangements made to escape the trap of arranged marriages so blissfully anticipated by the young men in poem 62.

The last interactive pair consists of the two outermost poems in the sequence, 61 and 68. Once again, we have striking thematic and metrical contrasts. In poem 61 Catullus explores the possibilities for erotic satisfaction offered by marriage. Beginning with an invocation to the god Hymen, "who / hastens the tender bride to her / bridegroom," the poem is structured as a wedding procession itself, which starts off in the house of the bride and ends in the house of her husband. Although Catullus allows himself numerous thematic and narrative digressions, the poem is centered on this procession. We first see the bride as she is preparing to set forth:

> Throw back the doorbolt, the bride is
> approaching! See how the torches
> shake out their flamboyant tresses!
> . . . .
> . . . . she
> lingers, becomingly modest;
> and looking back to her childhood,
> weeps at having to leave it.   [76–78, 82–85]

The procession of the bride to her husband's house takes place under cover, as it were, of various digressions on such topics as the sexual satisfactions that the husband will enjoy and the bride's enhanced status as mistress of a wealthy household. Eventually, the procession arrives at the house of her new husband, where the poet directs her to

> Cross the threshold in your golden
> slippers for a lucky omen,
> and pass through the polished doorway   [166–168]

We last see the married couple together on the wedding couch,
presumably about to take the poet's advice:

> Be good to
> each other, O newly wed pair:
> to work now, work at the constant
> task of practicing pleasure!   [232–235]

Poem 61 is an emotionally uncomplicated celebration of
marriage as a state of utter bliss. Poem 68, on the other hand,
is nothing if not complicated. Some of its complications derive
from the unanswered questions that I mentioned earlier: Is this
one poem or two? To whom is it addressed? To these questions
and to others that have engaged scholars over the years, there
are no canonical answers, and it may be that no such answers
are possible. Other complications arise from the poem's structure, which is chiastic and associative at the same time, allowing the poet to weave in a number of necessary digressions.
One is the story of Laodamia and Protesilaus, whose marriage,
unsanctified by a necessary sacrifice, ended when Protesilaus
became the first to fall at Troy. His death reminds Catullus of
his brother's unhappy fate, and Laodamia stands as a model
against which women in love may be judged.

Complexities of transmission and structure aside, I think
that some light can be thrown on the poet's intentions in poem
68 by reading it as one of a thematically opposed pair of poems,
the other being poem 61: as an epithalamion is to married life,
so poem 68 is to adultery. The epithalamion offers us an
idealized view of the satisfactions of marriage, from which
even the possibility of adultery is banished; in poem 68 Catullus makes a realistic assessment of the satisfactions possible
in an adulterous relationship, and, not surprisingly, they turn
out to be almost as good as—if not superior to—those of
marriage.

Although other readings are possible, I think it makes
sense to read poem 68 as a single entity consisting of two separate but closely related poems written to the same person,
whose identity is now unknown. (But what delicious Catullan

comedy if it were—as it might possibly be—the same husband as in poem 61, Manlius Torquatus!) The first part is a response to his correspondent, who has asked him for gifts of verse and especially of love poetry, a consolation for present unhappiness caused by either the death or the estrangement of his mistress. Catullus replies that the death of his brother has left him indifferent to love and incapable of poetry. He ends with an assurance of his affection for his correspondent. After this apparent conclusion, the poem abruptly starts up again like someone suddenly awakened from a nap:

> Muses, I can't remain silent concerning the matter
> in which I was so greatly aided by Allius— [41–42]

A few lines later, Catullus reveals the nature of the favor his correspondent provided:

> He gave me access, a path to a field once forbidden,
> he gave me a house and gave me its mistress also,
> and in that place we explored our mutual passion.
> There my radiant goddess appeared to me, stepping
> lightly and paused once—to stand with the sole of her
> sandal
> on the well-worn threshold as her bright foot crossed
> it [67–72]

In poem 61, the bride leaves the house of her father to come to the house of her husband; the procession is the poem. Poem 68, while more complicated in its structure than poem 61, is about an analogous but contrastive process; a wife leaves the house of her husband to come to the house that the poet's friend has made available to the poet and his mistress for their adulterous liaison. In poem 61 the bride was accompanied by those who were in charge of her; at the threshold of the husband's house, Catullus tells them,

> No need to lead her inside now,
> let go of her smooth arm, let her
> come to the couch of her husband. [181–183]

This would ordinarily have been the duty of her father. In poem 68, Catullus recalls a different situation:

> Nor was she brought to me on the right hand of her
>   father,
>   out of a house made fragrant with Syrian incense,
> but in the marvelous nighttime she came with those
>   precious
>   gifts she'd stolen right from the lap of her husband!
>   [145–148]

Nevertheless, Catullus is eager to bring out certain parallels between the two situations: the bride crosses the threshold in her golden slippers, the mistress pauses with the sole of her sandal on the threshold—what kind of omen was that, one wonders? The bride is attended by the god Hymen, dressed in yellow, and the mistress appears accompanied by Cupid, clothed in similar hue. But before her appearance, Catullus has been praising Laodamia for the ardor of her passion. Now, turning to the subject of his mistress, he remarks,

> My darling lacked little or nothing of [Laodamia's]
>   perfection
>   when she brought herself to lie in my embraces,
> for Cupid was there and constantly flitted about her,
>   the god resplendent in his bright saffron tunic!
>   [131–134]

Poems 61 and 68 were intended to mirror one another. Poem 68 deliberately reverses the journey by which the virgin is brought forth from the house of her father and led to the house of her husband; when we first see the mistress, she is arriving at the house of assignation, and our last glimpse is of her leaving the lap of her husband. If poem 61 promises a return to the Age of Gold, poem 68 reveals the satisfactions possible in the present. Fidelity is not one of them, but this does not bother the poet:

So, if she must have others besides her Catullus, we'll
     suffer
   the infrequent lapses of our artful lady
   lest we should too much resemble respectable people
. . . .
So it is really enough if she saves for us only
   those days which she marks with the white stone of
      celebration   [135–137, 149–150]

We ought to take the poet at his word here; poem 68 is more
worldly and self-assured in its values than it gets credit for. It
is about the pleasures and sorrows of adultery, not about how
much better marriage is than adultery. Laodamia and Protesilaus serve as emblems of one of the problems with marriage:
what happens if the commitment for life is abruptly termi-
nated by the death of one partner or the other?

My title for this chapter contains something of a teaser:
have we at last found the poet's fingerprints on the arrangement of his Book? Only Catullus could have provided the sym-
metrical, chiastic structure of poem 64; the extension of that
structure into the poems surrounding it seems to me just as
plausibly the work of the poet himself: such a design must exist
before the poems that embody it and therefore must be the
work of the poet rather than of his editor.

The existence of such a structure surely has implications
for reading the poems themselves. Although the conclusion of
poem 68 is triumphantly and unreservedly in favor of opportunistic adultery, this does not indicate that Catullus has given
up on the possibilities of marriage and opted wholly for the
pleasures of limited commitment. In a chiastic sequence, balance is everything. Poems find their meaning in the sequence
not by the argument they make but by their place in the design
that the entire sequence proposes. Marriage has its place, and
so do the ungovernable obsessions of our erotic life. There is
no argument being made in the sequence as whole, and if there
were, then Catullus would probably have had to find an al-

together different structure for it. One might argue that the sequence darkens as it progresses, but even so, Catullus is careful to maintain the delicate balance; the horror in poem 63 against the idealism of poems 61 and 62, the optimism of poem 66 against the disenchantment of poems 67 and 68. The structure of the sequence itself supports balanced acceptance rather than judgmental exclusion. It seems to me possible that the influences of that structure might radiate outward from poem 64 in the center, beyond poems 61–68, into the enchanting polymetric poems on one side and the disenchanting elegiacs on the other, infusing the Book of Catullus with a complex unity.

Catullus differs from the other figures examined in the Hermes series in two important ways: one is his accessibility to the general reader, and the other is his relative lack of influence on our literary culture before the beginning of the modern era. While Horace, Virgil, and Ovid shaped our poetic meters and matters, Catullus lay hidden under his bushel. Discovered (as a source of influence) by the Victorians and championed by the early modernists, he is now in a real sense one of us, a Latin poet who speaks to our age with a singular directness.

And yet, even if we think of Catullus as a contemporary, we ought to avoid thinking that we have absorbed him, that we have understood him completely. We admire his independence, his variety, and his virtuosity; we are, I think, well on the way to recognizing his passionate cerebrality. And yet there are important aspects of his work that have so far been slighted. I am thinking in particular of the elaborate complexity of his experiments in form in the longer poems, and of the corresponding spirit of playfulness and comic invention in the shorter ones. There is a sense in which we have overlooked some of the possibilities his poetry offers for an art of independence, variety, virtuosity, self-awareness, elegant form, comic invention. . . .

It is difficult, as Catullus says, to end a long affair. Nevertheless, I am reconciled to leaving his work at this point, in the certainty that future readers will discover in him an as yet unexhausted influence on the present: the little book that outlasted his age is just as likely to outlast ours.

NOTES

Preface

1. R. G. C. Levens, "Catullus," *Approaches to Catullus*, Kenneth Quinn, ed. (Cambridge: Heffer, 1972), 5.

I. "The Very Worst of Poets"

Note to Epigraph: Eric Havelock, *The Lyric Genius of Catullus* (New Haven: Yale University Press, 1967), 93.

1. Horace, Odes III, 30, ll. 1–5, my translation.

2. Clifford Geertz, "Stir Crazy," *New York Review of Books*, 24, nos. 21–22 (January 26, 1978), 3.

3. Archibald MacLeish, "Ars Poetica," in *New and Collected Poems* (Boston: Houghton Mifflin, 1976), 106.

4. Wallace Stevens, "Of Modern Poetry," in *The Collected Poems of Wallace Stevens* (New York: Alfred A. Knopf, 1965), 259.

5. Walter de la Mare, "All That's Past," in *Selected Poems*, R. N. Green-Armytage, ed. (London: Faber and Faber, 1954).

6. Ezra Pound, "L'Art, 1910," in *Personae of Ezra Pound* (New York: New Directions, 1926), 113.

7. William Carlos Williams, *Spring And All* (Buffalo: Frontier Press, 1970), 1–2.

8. Ezra Pound's view in *Literary Essays of Ezra Pound* (New York: New Directions, 1968), 240.

9. A. L. Wheeler, *Catullus and the Traditions of Ancient Poetry* (Berkeley: University of California Press, 1964), 41.

10. Ibid., 74.

11. Ibid., 258, n. 39.

12. Philodemus, book V, 43. *Greek Anthology*, vol. 1, ed. W. R. Paton, Loeb Classical Library, 1916, 150–151. All other quotations from Philodemus are from F. A. Wright, "Philodemus the Epicurean," *Edinburgh Review* 237 (January–April 1923), 306–318.

13. Callimachus, "Prologue to the *Aetia*, book 1, ll. 1–40, C. A. Trypanis, ed. and trans., Loeb Classical Library, 1958, 4–9.

14. Ezra Pound and F. S. Flint in Christopher Middleton, "Documents on Imagism from the Papers of F. S. Flint," *The Review* 15 (April 1965), 35–51.

15. J. W. H. Atkins, *Literary Criticism in Antiquity* (Gloucester: Peter Smith, 1961), 2: 56.

II. The Book of Catullus

Note to Epigraph: Yvor Winters, *Forms of Discovery* (Chicago: Swallow, 1967), 325.

1. Suetonius, *Lives of the Twelve Caesars,* Joseph Gavorse, ed. (New York: Random House, 1935), 40.

2. C. J. Fordyce, *Catullus: A Commentary* (London: Oxford University Press, 1961), preface (unpaged).

3. Wheeler, 19.

4. Ibid., 24.

5. Ulrich von Wilamowitz-Mollendorff, cited by Kenneth Quinn, *Catullus: An Interpretation* (New York: Harper & Row, 1973), 1.

6. Wheeler, 5–6.

7. Alexander Pope, "Epistle to a Lady," l. 247, in "Moral Essays" in *The Poems of Alexander Pope* (New Haven: Yale University Press, 1963), 568.

III. Life into Art

Note to Epigraph: W. H. Auden, "Who's Who," *Collected Poems,* Edward Mendelson, ed. (New York: Random House, 1991), 126.

1. Wheeler, 106.

2. E. T. Merrill, *Catullus* (Cambridge: Harvard University Press, 1982), xxv.

3. Sappho: *Greek Lyric,* vol. 1, David Campbell, trans. (Cambridge: Harvard University Press, 1982), 55.

IV. Of Poetry and Playfulness

Note to Epigraph: Frank O'Hara, "Personism: A Manifesto," in *The Collected Poems of Frank O'Hara* (New York: Alfred A. Knopf, 1971), 498.

1. Ezra Pound, "Tenzone," in *Personae of Ezra Pound,* 81.

2. William Butler Yeats, "Three Movements," in *The Collected Poems of William Butler Yeats* (New York: Macmillan, 1956), 236.

3. William Carlos Williams, *Paterson* (New York: New Directions, 1963), 28.

4. O'Hara, 498.

5. Merrill, 95.

6. G. P. Goold, *Catullus* (London: Duckworth, 1983), 248.

7. Gregory Bateson, "A Theory of Play and Fantasy," in *Steps to an Ecology of Mind* (San Francisco: Chandler, 1972), 177–193. All quotations from Bateson in chapter IV are from this essay.

8. Merrill, 211.

V. Invitations and Excoriations

1. Wheeler, 3.

2. Wilhelm Kroll, cited in Kenneth Quinn, *The Catullus Revolution* (Ann Arbor: University of Michigan Press, 1959), 30.

3. Merrill, xxxii.

4. William Butler Yeats, "The Scholars," in *Collected Poems of Yeats*, 139.

5. Quinn, *Catullan Revolution*, 32.

6. Horace, Odes I, 5.

7. Wallace Stevens, "The Pleasures of Merely Circulating," in *Collected Poems of Wallace Stevens*, 149.

8. Horace, "Art of Poetry," in *Criticism: The Major Texts*, Walter Jackson Bate, ed. (New York: Harcourt, Brace, 1952), 53.

9. Horace, Odes III, 30, ll. 1–2.

10. Stevens, in *Collected Poems of Wallace Stevens*, 239.

VI. Transformations of the Gift

Note to Epigraph: Marianne Moore, "The Past Is the Present," *The Complete Poems of Marianne Moore* (New York: Viking, 1967), 88.

1. Propertius, Book 2, poem 34, ll. 88–90.

2. Cicero, "Pro Caelio," 10, *Cicero: The Speeches*, R. Gardner, trans. Loeb Classical Library, 1965, 469.

3. Wallace Stevens, "The Emperor of Ice Cream," in *Collected Poems of Wallace Stevens*, 64.

4. Ezra Pound, *The Cantos of Ezra Pound* (London: Faber and Faber, 1964), 568.

VII. On Passionate Virtuosity in a Poem of Some Length

Note to Epigraph: John Barth, quoted on the dust jacket of *Lost in the Funhouse: Fiction for Print, Tape, Live Voice* (New York: Doubleday, 1968).

1. S. N. Behrman, in *Portrait of Max* (New York: Random House, 1960), 115.

2. Italo Calvino, *Six Memos for the Next Millennium* (Cambridge: Harvard University Press, 1988), 86.

3. Milan Kundera, *The Book of Laughter and Forgetting* (New York: Penguin, 1981), 232.

4. Wallace Stevens, *Opus Posthumous* (New York: Alfred A. Knopf, 1957), 160.

VIII. Lifting the Poet's Fingerprints

1. Fordyce, 262.

BIBLIOGRAPHY

GIVEN THE AIMS OF THIS SERIES, I HAVE TRIED TO LIST THE ITEMS BELOW in the likely order a student of Catullus, whether in or out of school, might find them useful.

The reader with little or no Latin will want an English version, preferably in verse. Catullus has often been translated into English, but few poetic translations are currently in print. The most recent entry in the field is mine: *The Poems of Catullus* (Baltimore, 1990) includes an introduction and notes on the poems. Peter Whigham's durable version is currently available from the University of California Press, *The Poems of Catullus* (Berkeley, 1983). A perennial favorite, Horace Gregory's early modernist translation, inspired by Ezra Pound's "Homage to Sextus Propertius," is currently out of print, as is James Michie's rhymed and metered version. Louis and Celia Zukofsky's *Poems of Catullus* (London, 1969) is perhaps more successful as an exploration of the range of possibilities for poetic translation than as a translation of Catullus.

The reader with a little Latin will need a text, a translation, and perhaps a commentary in order to begin reading Catullus. The Loeb Classical Library edition, *Catullus, Tibullus, and Pervigilium Veneris* (Cambridge, Mass., 1962), is widely available, but it lacks a commentary, and there probably has not been a century in the last millennium or so during which its prose translation would not have seemed quaintly archaic. The edition by G. P. Goold, *Catullus* (London, 1983), provides both a serviceable translation and an interesting commentary. The reader with enough Latin to dispense with a translation will want David H. Garrison's *Student's Catullus* (Norman, Okla., 1989), which comes with an introduction, notes, and several useful appendixes. It might well be supplemented by Stuart G. P. Small's helpful survey, *Catullus: A Reader's Guide to the Poems* (Lanham, Md., 1983).

The commentaries in the editions of Catullus by E. T. Merrill (Cambridge, Mass., 1982), C. J. Fordyce (London, 1961), and Kenneth Quinn (London, 1970) remain very useful.

Although most books about Catullus address the concerns of his professional students, there are some distinguished exceptions. A. L. Wheeler's *Catullus and the Traditions of Ancient Poetry* (Berkeley, 1964) is still a highly readable and reliable guide to the poems in their classical context. Eric Havelock's *Lyric Genius of Catullus*, first published in 1939 and reissued by Yale University Press in 1967, offers a selection of verse translations and a discussion of Catullus as a lyric poet. Kenneth Quinn's *Catullan Revolution* (Ann Arbor, 1959) offers a concise description of the poet in his time and a critical reading of the poetry for ours; Professor Quinn's *Catullus: An Interpretation* (New York, 1973) is a less concise, more contentious attempt to answer some of the enduring Catullan questions. *Catullus and His World* by T. P. Wiseman (Cambridge, 1985) is an often exciting collection of essays on the poems, their author, and the figures of note surrounding him.

Many of these have been long-term companions, here gratefully remembered; all can be recommended to the reader for whom the Hermes Books are intended.

INDEX

Abuse by iambic verse, 28–29. *See also* Poetic abuse
Acrostic, 83
Aemilius, 77–78, 81, 138–39, 144
Aeneas, 153
Aesop, 118
Alexandrian poets: as influence on neoterics, 13–18, 92, 93; view of poetry, 17, 22–23; and playfulness, 72
Allius, Manius, 173
Ambiguity, 81–83
Ameana, 60–64
Andronicus, Livius, 11, 13
Apuleius, 44
Ariadne, 151–53, 158, 161–65, 171
Aristotle, 22, 114, 152
Arrius, 85–86
Art, Roman, 154–56
Asinius, Marrucinus, 99, 126–27, 130, 132
Attis, 54–55, 172, 175–76
Auden, W. H., 114
Audience: for poetry, 5–11, 67; for Catullus' poetry, 10–11, 67, 116–17, 151
Aurelius, 59–60, 76–79, 141–42
Autonomy, 115–16

Barth, John, 153, 154
Bateson, Gregory, 73–75, 76, 81
Beerbohm, Max, 152
Bibaculus, Furius, 19
Bithynia, journey to, 45, 46–47, 103, 123, 124, 146
Book of Catullus, 26, 31–33

Caecilius, 19, 38, 98, 102–03, 152

Caelius, 64
Caesar, Julius, 28–29, 35, 38, 39, 41, 60, 62, 99, 119
Callimachus, 15–18, 20, 90, 131, 172, 177
Calvino, Italo, 153, 154
Calvus, Licinius: and Cicero, 18, 20; as neoteric, 19, 27; composing poetry with Catullus, 27, 32, 69, 70; gift to Catullus, 128–29, 130, 131; author of *Io*, 152
Camerius, 99, 133–34
Campesani, Benvenuto, 31
Catiline, 41
Cato, M. Porcius, 38
Cato, Valerius, 19, 38
Catullus, Gaius Valerius:
—life of: birth, 39; death, 39; in Verona, 39–40; death of brother, 40, 45–46, 53, 88–91, 123, 145–47, 181; education, 40–41; in Rome, 40–41; villa at Sirmione, 40; villa near Tivoli, 40; and Lesbia, 41–45, 47–64, 73, 85, 86–88, 101–02, 105–12, 143, 145; journey to Bithynia, 45, 46–47, 103, 123, 124, 146;
—as poet: and the classics, 3–5; contributions of, 5, 184–85; as neoteric, 5; Alexandrians as influence on, 13–18, 92, 93; Roman predecessors as influence on, 15; habits of composition, 26–27, 69–70;
—poems of: audience for, 10–11, 27–28, 67, 116–17, 151; gift-giving as theme in, 10, 33, 122–23, 124–36; Book of Catullus as collected

Catullus—poems of (*continued*)
poems and as canon, 26, 31–33;
discussion and performance of,
27; poetic abuse in, 28–29, 44–45,
57–64, 76–81, 103–04, 137–39,
145; contemporary response to,
29, 151; survival of, 29–32; arrangement of, 32–36; elegiac
poems, 32, 34, 36, 84–91; length
as criteria for arrangement of, 32;
long poems, 32, 33; metrical criteria for arrangement of, 32; polymetric poems, 32, 33, 34, 35, 36,
83, 84; poet's responsibility for arrangement of, 33–34; relation of
arrangement to criticism of, 34;
chiasmus as structure in, 35–36,
157–58, 172–84; social nature of,
37, 88–91, 99, 122; playfulness of,
76–84, 144–45, 184; obscenity in,
77–78, 80, 103–04, 121, 122, 137–
39, 143–44; exaggeration in, 79–
80; ambiguity in, 81–83; clarifica-
tion of mysterious situation as
theme in, 84–86; composing as art
in, 88–91; sensibility as divided
in, 92–94; self-consciousness of,
93–94; "two-Catullus" theory, 93;
poem-as-invitation, 98–106, 106–
20; dialogue and invitation, 100–
06; excoriation in, 103–05; autonomy, 115–16; spectatorship for,
116–17; abruptness of beginning
of, 117; conclusions of, 117–19;
homecoming as theme of, 123–24;
conviviality as theme of, 130–32;
theft and, 131–32; silence and,
134–35; reading of poems *61–68*
based on chiastic structure, 172–84;
—poem *64*: 151–53, 156–71; summary of, 152–53; influence of visual artists on, 154–56; length of,
156; structure of, 156–58, 171; as
continuous narrative, 157, 158;
chiastic structure in, 157–58; visual elements in, 158–63, 171;
convergence in, 160–61, 163–65,
167–70; dispersal and destruction
in, 166–70; as mystery, 170–71; relation to surrounding poems,
174–75
Celer, Quintus Metellus, 43, 45

Chiasmus: as principle of arrangement of poems, 35–36, 80; reading of poems *61–68* based on,
172–84
Cicero: and Calvus, 18, 20; and neoterics, 18; as champion of classics,
18, 69, 71; and Catullus, 38, 39,
41; and Clodia, 44; Catullus'
poem addressed to, 83; description of smart set, 99, 130
Cinna, Gaius Helvius, 19, 21–22, 46,
151–52
Classics: and Catullus, 3–5; Latin
translations of, 11–12, 13. *See also*
names of specific authors
Clodia Metelli, 38, 43, 44–45, 47
Codex, 31
Codex Veronensis, 32
Convergence, in poem *64*, 160–61,
163–65, 167–70
Conviviality, as theme of poems,
130–32
Cornificius, 19
Cybele, 54, 59, 152, 172, 175–76

Dante, 31, 156
Darwin, Charles, 5
De la Mare, Walter, 8
Death, associated with sexuality,
135–39
Depth, illusion of, 155–56, 159–60,
171
Dialogue to invitation, 100–06
Dispersal, in poem *64*, 166–70

Eating, associated with sexuality,
135–39, 140, 142
Elegiac poems, 32, 34, 36, 84–91
Eliot, T. S., 37, 92
Ennius, Quintus, 13, 14, 20, 21
Epics: first Roman epic, 13, 21;
Cinna's *Zmyrna*, 21–22, 151–52;
expectations for, 152; Homeric
epic, 154
Epyllion, 151–53, 172
Eratosthenes, 23, 72
Eroticism. *See* Sexuality
Exaggeration, 79–80, 82, 114
Excoriation, 103–05

Fabullus, 47, 98, 112–15, 127–28,
130, 131, 135

Flavius, 99, 132–34, 142
Flint, F. S., 20
Fordyce, C. J., 177
Foucault, Michel, 5
Freud, Sigmund, 5
Furius, 59–60, 76–79, 142, 143

Geertz, Clifford, 4–5
Gellius, Aulus, 15, 27, 62, 84, 137
Gift-giving: as theme in Catullan
    poetry, 10, 33, 122–23, 124–32;
    and conviviality, 130–32; and
    theft, 131–32; and silence, 132–34;
    transformation of gifts, 134–36
Goold, G. P., 72, 83
Grief, at death of Catullus' brother,
    40, 45–46, 53, 88–91, 123, 145–47,
    181

Hannibal, 39
Hemingway, Ernest, 26
Homecoming, as theme of poetry,
    123–24
Homer, 20, 155
Homoerotic attachment to young
    boy, 122, 139–45
Homosexual rape, threat of, 59–60,
    76–79
Horace, 3, 4, 30, 68, 94–98, 116–19,
    184
Hortensius, 21

Imagination, in poetry, 23–25, 112–
    14
Invitation, poem as: examples of,
    98–100, 112–14; negative invita-
    tions, 99; dialogue and, 100–06;
    excoriation and, 103–05; interior
    monologue and, 106–12; polyph-
    ony and, 106–12; imagination
    and, 112–14; and conclusion of
    poems, 117–19; provisionality and
    mobility of, 119–20
Ipsitilla, 99, 101, 112, 115, 135–36

Johnson, Dr. Samuel, 47
Juventius, 80, 84–85, 121–22, 139–45

Kroll, Wilhelm, 92
Kundera, Milan, 154

Laevius, 15, 72

Lesbia: identity of, 38–39, 43, 44–45,
    47; purpose of pseudonym for,
    41–45; as poet, 44; poems mythol-
    ogizing relationship, 48, 53–56;
    poems of courtship, 48–53; poet's
    dismissal of, 48, 57–59, 62–64, 87–
    88, 106–12, 137, 143, 145; poet's
    self-conscious analysis of relation-
    ship, 48, 55–57, 86; compared
    with Ameana, 61–62; ambiguity
    and exaggeration in poems about,
    82–83; mysterious situation clari-
    fied concerning, 85, 86–87; invita-
    tion to, 98, 101–02, 115; poet's
    desire for invitation from, 105–06;
    fame of, 121
Lowell, Robert, 37
Lucretius, 46

MacLeish, Archibald, 6, 7
Mallius, Allius, 173
Mamurra, 28–29, 35, 60, 62–64, 99
Marriage, compared with erotic pas-
    sion, 174–83
Marsh, Edwin, 7
Martial, 33
Memmius, Gaius, 13, 39, 41, 46, 47,
    103–04
Merrill, E. T., 46–47, 72, 81, 92
Metacommunicative discourse, 73–
    74, 77
Metafiction, 153–54
Miller, Henry, 4
Mimesis, 114
Monroe, Harriet, 20
Moore, Marianne, 122

Naevius, 13
Neoteric poets: concerns of, 5, 20–
    21, 69, 71, 153, 155; Alexandrian
    poets as influence on, 13–18; as
    tightly knit coterie, 18–19; mem-
    bers of, 19–20
Nepos, Cornelius, 33, 122, 130, 134
Neptolemus, 24

Obscenity, 77–78, 80, 103–04, 121,
    122, 137–39, 143–44. See also Sex-
    uality
O'Hara, Frank, 70, 83
Ortalus, 88–91

Ovid, 14, 68, 184

Papyrus, 31
Patron-client model, 12–13
Payne, Robert, 4
Peleus, 151, 153, 165, 170
Persephone, 146
Philodemus, 13, 16–17, 19, 23–24, 30, 64, 122
Picasso, Pablo, 155
Piso, L. Calpurnius, 23, 41
Plato, 22
Plautus, 13, 14
Playfulness: and poetry, 71–73; and metacommunicative discourse, 73–74, 77; Bateson's paradigm of, 73–75, 76, 81; as paradox, 74–75; in poetry of Catullus, 76–84, 144–45, 184; exaggeration and, 79–80, 82; ambiguity and, 81–83
Poem-as-invitation: examples of, 98–100, 112–14; negative invitations, 99; dialogue and, 100–06; excoriation and, 103–05; interior monologue and, 106–12; polyphony and, 106–12; imagination and, 112–14; and conclusion of poems, 117–19; provisionality and mobility of, 119–20
Poem-as-souvenir, 94–98
Poem 64. See Catullus, Gaius Valerius, poem 64
Poetic abuse, 28–29, 44–45, 57–64, 76–81, 103–04, 137–39, 145
Poetry: audience for, 5–11, 67; early Roman poetry, 11; and patron-client model, 12–13; influence of Alexandrians on, 13–18; as public affair, 14; social nature of, 14, 67, 88–91, 99; Alexandrian concept of, 17, 22–23; neoterics' view of, 20–21; Aristotle's view of, 22, 114; Plato's view of, 22; Stoics' view of, 22, 72; didactic nature of, 23, 30, 72; imagination in, 23–25; composing as art, 68–71; playfulness and, 71–73; and imagination, 112–14. See also names of specific poets
Polymetric poems, 32, 33, 34, 35, 36, 83, 84
Polyphony, 106–12, 154
Polyxena, 169–70

Pompey, 38
Pope, Alexander, 35, 77
Porphyrio, 15
Pound, Ezra, 4, 7–8, 13–14, 20, 67, 92, 147, 155
Propertius, 14, 44, 68
Pulcher, Publius Clodius, 38, 39, 44

Quinn, Kenneth, 93–94, 115
Quintius, 85

Ravidus, 28
Rufa, 136–37, 142
Rufus, 84, 120
Rufus, Caelius, 64
Rufus, Marcus Caelius, 130

Sappho, 14, 20, 42, 44, 48, 49, 50
Scala, Can Grande della, 31
Schliemann, Heinrich, 4
Sexuality: threat of homosexual rape, 59–60, 76–79; erotic nature of composition of poetry, 70–71, 89; homoerotic attachment to young boy, 122, 139–45; eating and death associated with, 135–39, 140, 142; sexuality rapacity, 135–39; fellatio, 137–38; love in marriage versus erotic passion, 174–83. See also Lesbia; Obscenity
Shakespeare, William, 19
Silence, 132–34
Souvenir, poem as, 94–98
Spartacus, 41
Spectatorship, 116–17
Stein, Gertrude, 155
Stevens, Wallace, 6–7, 112, 136, 154
Stoics, 22, 72
Suetonius, 29, 37
Suffenus, 118
Sulla, 131

Terence, 13, 14
Thallus, 131–32
Theft, 131–32
Theseus, 151–53, 163, 165, 171
Thetis, 151, 153, 165, 170
Tibullus, 44
Ticidas, 44
Torquatus, Manlius, 172, 173
"Two-Catullus" theory, 93

Vanishing line, 156

Varus, 103–05, 122, 129
Veranius, 47, 119–20, 122, 131
Vibennius and Son, 99, 138, 144
Virgil, 4, 30, 153, 184
Volusius, 21

Wheeler, A. L., 15, 33, 34, 38, 92

Wilamowitz–Mollendorff, Ulrich
   von, 33–34
Wilder, Thornton, 38
Williams, William Carlos, 4, 9, 10,
   67, 155

Yeats, William Butler, 35, 67, 92